## BEFORE YOU START READING, DOWNLOAD YOUR FREE BONUSES!

Click the link or scan the QR-code & access all the resources for FREE!

**https://dl.bookfunnel.com/h8hzy33mn7**

## The Self-Sufficient Living Cheat Sheet

## 10 Simple Steps to Become More Self-Sufficient in 1 Hour or Less

How to restore balance to the environment around you... even if you live in a tiny apartment in the city.

Discover:

- **How to increase your income** by selling "useless" household items
- The environmentally friendly way to replace your car — invest in THIS special vehicle to **eliminate your carbon footprint**
- The secret ingredient to **turning your backyard into a thriving garden**
- 17+ different types of food scraps and 'waste' that you can use to feed your garden
- How to drastically **cut down on food waste** without eating less
- 4 natural products you can use to make your own eco-friendly cleaning supplies
- The simple alternative to 'consumerism' — the age-old method for **getting what you need without paying money for it**
- The 9 fundamental items you need to create a self-sufficient first-aid kit
- One of the top skills that most people are afraid of learning — and how you can master it effortlessly
- 3 essential tips for **gaining financial independence**

# The Prepper Emergency Preparedness & Survival Checklist:

## 10 Easy Things You Can Do Right Now to Ready Your Family & Home for Any Life-Threatening Catastrophe

**Natural disasters demolish everything in their path, but your peace of mind and sense of safety don't have to be among them. Here's what you need to know…**

- Why having an emergency plan in place is so crucial and how it will help to keep your family safe
- How to stockpile emergency supplies intelligently and why you shouldn't overdo it
- How to store and conserve water so that you know you'll have enough to last you through the crisis
- A powerful 3-step guide to ensuring financial preparedness, no matter what happens
- A step-by-step guide to maximizing your storage space, so you and your family can have exactly what you need ready and available at all times
- Why knowing the hazards of your home ahead of time could save a life and how to steer clear of these in case of an emergency
- Everything you need to know for creating a successful evacuation plan, should the worst happen and you need to flee safely

## 101 Recipes, Tips, Crafts, DIY Projects and More for a Beautiful Low Waste Life

## Reduce Your Carbon Footprint and Make Earth-Friendly Living Fun With This Comprehensive Guide

Practical, easy ways to improve your personal health and habits while contributing to a brighter future for yourself and the planet

Discover:

- **Simple customizable recipes for creating your own food, home garden, and skincare products**
- The tools you need for each project to successfully achieve sustainable living
- Step-by-step instructions for life-enhancing skills from preserving food to raising your own animals and forging for wild berries
- **Realistic life changes that reduce your carbon-footprint while saving you money**
- Sustainable crafts that don't require any previous knowledge or expertise
- Self-care that extends beyond the individual and positively impacts the environment
- **Essential tips on how to take back control of your life -- become self-sustained and independent**

## First Aid Fundamentals

## A Step-By-Step Illustrated Guide to the Top 10 Essential First Aid Procedures Everyone Should Know

Discover:

- **What you should do to keep this type of animal attack from turning into a fatal allergic reaction**
- Why sprains are more than just minor injuries, and how you can keep them from getting worse
- **How to make the best use of your environment in critical situations**
- The difference between second- and third-degree burns, and what you should do when either one happens
- Why treating a burn with ice can actually cause more damage to your skin
- When to use heat to treat an injury, and when you should use something cold
- **How to determine the severity of frostbite**, and what you should do in specific cases
- Why knowing this popular disco song could help you save a life
- The key first aid skill that everyone should know — **make sure you learn THIS technique the right way**

# Food Preservation Starter Kit

## 10 Beginner-Friendly Ways to Preserve Food at Home | Including Instructional Illustrations and Simple Directions

Grocery store prices are skyrocketing! It's time for a self-sustaining lifestyle.

Discover:

- **10 incredibly effective and easy ways to preserve your food for a self-sustaining lifestyle**
- The art of canning and the many different ways you can preserve food efficiently without any prior experience
- A glorious trip down memory lane to learn the historical methods of preservation passed down from one generation to the next
- **How to make your own pickled goods**: enjoy the tanginess straight from your kitchen
- Detailed illustrations and directions so you won't feel lost in the preservation process
- The health benefits of dehydrating your food and how fermentation can be **the key to a self-sufficient life**
- **The secrets to living a processed-free life** and saving Mother Earth all at the same time

**Download All the resources by clicking this link or scanning the QR-Code below:**

https://dl.bookfunnel.com/n15biloqb9

# MARKET GARDENING

*Step-By-Step Guide to Start Your Own Small
Scale Organic Farm in as Little as 30 Days
Without Stress or Extra work*

SMALL FOOTPRINT PRESS

## © Copyright 2021 - All rights reserved.

The content contained within this book may not be reproduced, duplicated, or transmitted without direct written permission from the author or the publisher.

Under no circumstances will any blame or legal responsibility be held against the publisher, or author, for any damages, reparation, or monetary loss due to the information contained within this book, either directly or indirectly.

Legal Notice:

This book is copyright protected. It is only for personal use. You cannot amend, distribute, sell, use, quote, or paraphrase any part, or the content within this book, without the consent of the author or publisher.

Disclaimer Notice:

Please note the information contained within this document is for educational and entertainment purposes only. All effort has been executed to present accurate, up-to-date, reliable, complete information. However, no warranties of any kind are declared or implied. Readers acknowledge that the author is not engaged in the rendering of legal, financial, medical, or professional advice. The content within this book has been derived from various sources. Please consult a licensed professional before attempting any techniques outlined in this book.

By reading this document, the reader agrees that under no circumstances is the author responsible for any losses, direct or indirect, that are incurred as a result of the use of the information contained within this document, including, but not limited to, errors, omissions, or inaccuracies.

# Table of Contents

Introduction ................................................................. 15
Chapter 1: Establishing Roots ................................... 19
    Rule Number One .................................................... 19
        Avoiding Debt ..................................................... 19
        Don't Learn The Hard Way ................................ 22
    Know Your Market ................................................. 25
        Market Now, Not Later ...................................... 26
        Know Your Land .................................................. 28
    Setting Realistic Goals ........................................... 29
        Align Goals With Your Passion ........................ 29
        Set Reasonable Goals ........................................ 31
Chapter 2: Understand the Risk vs. Reward ............ 35
    The Pros ................................................................... 36
        Welcome to Entrepreneurship ........................ 36
        Maintain a Healthier Lifestyle ......................... 36
        Predictable Demand .......................................... 37
        Easy Diversification ........................................... 38
        Gratitude and Life Satisfaction ....................... 38
    The Cons .................................................................. 40
        Mother Nature ..................................................... 40
        The Workday Feels Like It Never Ends ......... 41
        Everything Is Your Responsibility ................. 42
        Financial Concerns ............................................ 42
    Weighing Your Options ......................................... 43
Chapter 3: Gathering the Essentials ......................... 46
    Land .......................................................................... 46
    Seeds ........................................................................ 47
        Seed Varieties ...................................................... 50

- Tools and Gear ............................................................. 51
- Larger Equipment ......................................................... 54
  - Tractor .................................................................... 54
  - Plows ..................................................................... 58
  - All-Terrain Vehicles (ATV) or Utility Vehicle (UTV) ............................................................ 58
  - Pickup Truck ......................................................... 59
  - Wagon or Trailer .................................................. 60
  - Cultivator .............................................................. 60
  - Cultipacker ........................................................... 61
  - Plastic Mulch Layer ............................................. 61
  - Irrigation System ................................................. 62
  - Seed Drills ............................................................ 62
  - Transplanter ........................................................ 63
  - Backhoe ................................................................ 64
  - Front-End Loader ................................................ 65
  - Harvester ............................................................. 65
  - Hay Balers and Rakes ......................................... 66
- Outsourcing .................................................................. 66
- Crafting the Right Business Plan ............................. 69
  - Drafting a Small Farm Business Plan ............. 71
- Chapter 4: Organize the Legal Side .............................. 78
  - Do You Have Enough Funds? ................................... 78
    - Grants .................................................................... 79
    - Loans ..................................................................... 82
    - Seed Money and Angel Investors .................... 86
  - Do You Have the Land? ............................................. 87
    - Licenses and Permits ......................................... 88
  - Do You Need Insurance? ........................................... 89
- Chapter 5: Know Your Seeds and What They'll Become ................................................................................ 94

- Choosing the Right Farm .......................................... 94
  - Types of Farms .................................................. 95
  - Profitable Crops to Consider ............................. 98
  - Seasonal Crops ................................................. 99
- Before You Start Planting ........................................ 100
  - Seeds vs. Starter Plants .................................. 100
  - Planting Techniques ........................................ 104
  - Seed Placement ............................................... 105
- Caring For Your Crops .............................................. 106
  - Pest Problems .................................................. 107
  - Tackle Weeds Early .......................................... 108

## Chapter 6: Caring For Your Land ............................ 109
- Fertilizing Your Soil ................................................. 109
- Organizing Your Land .............................................. 110
  - Tilling Practices ............................................... 111
  - Proper Sun Exposure ...................................... 113
  - Water Concerns ............................................... 114
- Soil Health and Nutrition ....................................... 116
  - Making Your Own Compost ........................... 116
  - Crop Rotations ................................................. 123
  - Cover Crops ...................................................... 124
  - Buffer Zones ..................................................... 125
- Growing and Staying Organic ................................ 126
  - Requirements for Organic Farms ................. 127
  - Being Certified ................................................. 129
- Time Investment ...................................................... 131

## Chapter 7: Prepping Your Crop for The Market .......... 132
- Is The Market Ready for You? ................................ 132
  - Do You Have Customers? ............................... 132
  - Build an Online Presence ............................... 133
- Proper Cleaning ........................................................ 135

- How To Sell? ........................................................... 136
  - Selling Locally .................................................... 136
  - Community-Supported Agriculture (CSA) ........... 137
  - Selling Wholesale ............................................... 138
  - Local Restaurants ............................................... 138
  - Trade Shows and Fairs ........................................ 139
  - Catalog Sales ...................................................... 140
- Delivering Products ............................................... 141
  - Establishing a Delivery Service .......................... 141
- Growing Your Business ........................................... 143
  - Reinvesting Your Profits ..................................... 144
  - Expand Your Reach ............................................. 145
  - Creating Effective Systems ................................. 145
  - Branding Yourself ............................................... 146
- Conclusion ................................................................. 148
- References ................................................................. 150

# Introduction

***"Growing Your Own Food is Like Printing Your Own Money"***

-Ron Finley

For many, buying a little house on wide stretches of land is a dream. People want to escape the non-stop hustle of city living and the exhausting days of working just for a paycheck. They want something more fulfilling to put their time, effort, and money into. There are many reasons why you may want to start your own farm and just as many reasons why you haven't yet. Maybe you do not have the money or the land. Maybe you have attempted to start small and saw nothing flourish from your efforts, and this keeps you from trying again.

You might be here because you are passionate about growing your own foods and creating a self-sustainable life. Perhaps you want to finally break free of the nine to five or 60 hour or more workweeks for a job that leaves you stressed and often depressed. Maybe the idea of having your own farm, whether to grow enough to feed your family or sell to generate an income, has been dancing around in your head for a while. With this in mind, you'll probably want to know how to take this thought and turn it into a reality, and a successful one at that.

If you don't know what you are getting into, it is easy to fail at starting your own farm. Some of you may have experienced this failure already with unsuccessful growing seasons. However, you can have the motivation, determination, and passion to try again and learn from your mistakes. You will just need to know the proper steps to take.

Farming is not for everyone. If you are looking for a quick way to earn a few extra bucks, this book may not be for you. If you just want tips to cut corners for fast, overnight results, you will not learn any of that on these pages. However, those who are willing to take action, put in the required effort, and make a commitment to continuously learn and grow as a farmer will find value in this book. This book was designed for people like you, with passion, drive, and a willingness to learn.

Small Footprint Press was created out of the same passion and drive that you have. We are a company dedicated to helping others learn how to live off their land by taking care of mother earth and its inhabitants. We are a team of enthusiastic professionals who have poured out time and effort into studying and reaching out to experts on sustainable living, prepping, living off-grid to create guides for individuals who are inspired to change their lifestyles. In addition, we have a love for all things outdoors, especially when it comes to building a better earth. It is from our passion that we feel compelled to share these amazing messages and information with others.

In the past year, we have been formulating books on the information we have collected from experts and our own research, on how to achieve a sustainable lifestyle that can allow any individual and their environment to thrive. Watching people in this world provide for themselves and their loved ones fills us with excitement. Seeing them accomplish their goals and living their purpose by creating their own farming business is what inspires us to get out of bed and help others to do the same. This is why we have carefully crafted this book, to help more people see the potential of their land and learn how to successfully care for it, so it may continue to give back for years.

The information in this book will provide you with a better insight into how to turn your small farm into a reliable source of income. Whether it is an acre, ten acres, or more, you will learn how you can grow and profit from what you have. There is so much more to operating a farm than just the crops and harvest. There are legal issues you can run into if you do not know what your small farming business needs. You will learn what insurance, permits, and other documents are necessary to run your farm legally. You will also have to learn about the marketing aspect of things and how you can better transform your passion into a business.

This book is not filled with information to read and forget. Instead, you will learn effective action plans that you can implement immediately. These plans are flexible and will provide you the structure, knowledge, and systems to grow a successful business. The sooner you get started, the sooner you will benefit, so let's start now. It is time to take the first step towards that dream of farm living you have always had.

# Chapter 1: Establishing Roots

Learning as much as you can from the beginning will put you in a position to make better, well-educated decisions on the operations of your farm. Effectively working on your farm will be lucrative, but it's easy to lose sight of important matters. So have patience and give yourself some credit as you embark on this journey. You will not become a master of every skill you need all at once. And at times no matter how much you plan and prepare, some things will not work out perfectly the first time.

## Rule Number One

Starting any business is a risk. While some businesses have lower risks, they can all lead to stress and financial strain. One of the things that you'll want to avoid is getting yourself in debt with no clear expectation of when you will make your initial investment back and start generating a profit. Deciding to start your own farm is highly rewarding, but without the right plan, it can cause you to lose a significant amount of money.

### *Avoiding Debt*

The startup cost for a new farmer will vary depending on what you already have to work with. If you already have the land, your cost of starting a farm can fall around $40,000, but most of these costs are essential investments that will make it possible for you to create a profit sooner, such as purchasing the right equipment. There are plenty of options for financing your small-scale farm, but even with funding, you need to spend wisely.

Spending sensibly requires you to make a budget and a plan. With these two components, you will make financial choices that get your agricultural business going without sinking into debt. For many beginners, this will mean having a great deal of patience. You will have to weigh the pros and cons of the many options you'll have at the beginning. You have to carefully consider the choices that will benefit you temporarily and those that will help you expand and reach your long-term goals sooner.

You may have to settle with used or borrowed equipment, ask family or friends for help, and research on how to do a lot of things yourself to save on money. This will keep you in safe financial standing. You never want to start spending money on things you can hold off on until you have enough capital to cover your overhead. Unfortunately, this may mean owning your own farm might have to be put on hold until you come up with your own savings to get started. This is a much better option. While you are saving, you can do the research and learn in the meantime, so that when you have the funds, you'll have a plan already in mind.

Incurring debt may be inevitable, and we will discuss funding options in greater detail in the next chapter. There are some ways to avoid getting stuck with a substantial amount of debt before you begin looking at your investment options. First, understand what types of debt you may encounter. These include:

- Secured
- Unsecured
- Fixed interest rates
- Variable interest rates
- Fixed payment term
- Variable payment term
- Deductible loans
- Non-deductible loans

Each of these has its own pros and cons. Choosing the right fit for your business will require a thorough evaluation of the direction you want your farm to go. Of course, being profitable is the main goal, but how you get there will influence the type of debt you might consider. A few things to avoid when it comes to choosing the right funding include:

- High-interest rates
- High late fees or penalties
- Obtaining a debt for things that will not increase your value or for things that have a short lifespan

- Relying too much on secured debt
- Unverified lending sources
- Obtaining debt that requires a monthly payment that is more than 36 percent of your gross monthly income

### *Don't Learn The Hard Way.*

It is okay to fail in some things. You will learn through the process. Amazingly, those in the agriculture industry like small farmers experience a much lower failure rate than those starting a business in the restaurant or other industries. This may or may not happen to you, but there are ways to make your chances better, by avoiding mistakes that have led others to fail. The following are things to be aware of as you begin and avoid as you continue to embark on this journey.

- Remember, your farm is your business. A mistake many beginners make is allowing the ideal of a farming lifestyle to impair their business sense. While the idea of growing your own food and maybe even raising some animals may look picturesque, this is not how you approach starting a successful business. As a business person, you need to carefully consider your market, profit margins, and products. You don't want to just grow some plants. You'll want to grow crops that you can sell, and this means you know what people want to buy that you can supply them. When you decide to start a farm, you will need to be clear as to whether you will be treating it like a business or a hobby.

- Easy and cheap will not build a sustainable business. As a beginner, it will be tempting to choose crops that are quick and easy to harvest and then turn around and sell these for a very low profit to compete against bigger chains. You may find a little bit of success with this approach, but most will waste a lot of time and energy only to achieve minimal success if any.

- Choose the right market. This connects to the first two points. You are operating a business, and to be successful, you will need to market to the right customer. You will need to see those who will be willing to spend on your produce and who will not just be looking for the lowest price. You do not want to compete with the local chain stores to sell your produce. It won't be possible for a small-scale farmer to capitalize on the same strategies as these chains. Instead, you will need to select profitable crops that are in demand and customers are willing to buy.

- Gain at least a basic understanding of your day-to-day accounting. If you have the means to hire an account, even better, but if it is only possible to handle the bigger financial obligation like taxes, then you will need to handle the accounting on your own. As a new business, it is vital to have a budget and know where your money is coming from and going towards. Do not get into the habit of buying your supplies without tracking what you are spending. By the end of the month, you will often have to sort out how bills and necessities will be paid the following month while still having to pay things off from the current month. You will have to understand what your cost of business is to understand what profits are possible.

- Have cash reserves. Farming is just like any other business, and you will be bound to encounter issues that will hit you hard financially. If you do not have a little cushion to get you through these hard hits, you will be completely out.

- Do not try to do everything. Have a clear vision of what you want for your farm and resist the urge to constantly have more, offer more, and undoubtedly will cost more. You will have to maintain a focus on what will turn the greatest profits, not what looks appealing, or you do not have any real interest in profiting.

- Do not try to mimic other successful farms unless you have a clear understanding of what makes them successful. Every farmer will have their own systems, marketing plan, and ways of doing business that have led them to success. Trying to copy what another farm is doing because they have had success does not mean you will have success. Most often, this will run right into failure. This does not mean you can not look to other well-established farmers for guidance or inspiration, but if you are trying to obtain the success of a farmer that produces grapes and apples while you are growing spinach and radish, you will not get the same results. If you want to implement what another farm is doing, first understand what it takes to implement that system. You might not be at the size or have the means to pursue that option yet.

## Know Your Market

How long should you wait until you begin marketing your future farm? You should not wait at all. If you are serious about establishing a successful business, you will need to start marketing that business before you even have the crops growing in the fields.

Marketing is grossly neglected by many farmers who are just starting out, and this is often the main reason their business grows only minimally, if at all. This is also the one aspect of business that intimidates entrepreneurs in many industries. If marketing makes you cringe, it is understandable. Many people have the wrong impression of what marketing is and should entail. Marketing your farm and products is not just about selling, which is where most entrepreneurs go wrong with their marketing approach. They try to push their products on people until they buy, and this is ineffective.

Marketing should be about sharing. Knowing what to share requires an understanding of your target market, but more importantly, it requires you to know why this is important to you. You do not need to have your farm yet. You do not need to be harvesting or packaging or anywhere near ready to start selling items. What you need is, to be honest and open about why you are starting a farm, what you want to gain, how you want to provide for your community and for your family. Sharing these personal reasons will attract the right people to your business. One important thing to do is to create a personality or branding that people can emotionally connect to. This should be done so that your customers won't see you only like a hungry salesman who only cares about making money, but as a human being that they can relate to, will want to listen to, and will want to support.

## *Market Now, Not Later*

Starting to share your story now creates interest and excitement about your future farm. You share with a few family and friends, start a social media page and share your journey with new followers, and before long, you'll have hundreds and maybe even thousands of people invested in your business. Although this can be a scary thought, these people will be following your journey as you make progress. They will feel like they are right there with you.

If you start marketing right away, you will begin to build strong relationships, and this creates loyal customers. Being transparent about your process will allow people to trust what you eventually end up providing. Sharing, instead of selling, allows people to follow along with you and learn more about who you are as a person, why this is important to you, and will allow them to start realizing that this is important to them too. For example, sharing that you are passionate about growing organic items because you want to eliminate potential chemicals you may be feeding to your family when you purchase store-bought, big chain produce will get followers rethinking what they feed to their families. Talking about how your small farm will have a positive impact on the environment will get people thinking about supporting local farmers more.

There are many topics you can cover and share that can resonate with your followers. Getting a headstart on this before you even have products to sell will ensure that you attract more than enough people who will then be just as passionate about seeing you succeed as you are. You can gain a great deal of support when you begin marketing by sharing first, instead of waiting to market just to sell. People are going to buy from what or who they know. By sharing your values or backstory, you can become someone they know personally and you can get a bump to the top of their buy-from list.

Social media has made it easier than ever to begin sharing now and gain attention. There are many ways you can approach social media marketing with your small farm. Each social media platform, like YouTube, Facebook, Instagram, and Twitter, have their own set of pros and cons. Each tends to cater to a specific demographic of users, and certain content, such as videos, images, or written text. Thus, each platform will perform differently. Obviously, YouTube is meant for video creators, while Facebook is ideal for those who can combine different types of content into one post.

You should start your plan on creating your social media accounts for your farming business now. You can begin with just one or two platforms to share regularly. You will also want to set up an email list and website and create a way to capture contact info for visitors. This will feel like a lot in the beginning as it can quickly become overwhelming, especially when you start adding all the daily tasks of preparing the land. But this is a vital component for your success. Creating a marketing or social media schedule will help you organize what you need to do daily and will allow you allocate a set time for getting these marketing responsibilities done.

### *Know Your Land*

This topic will be more thoroughly discussed in Chapter 5, but it is something many farmers feel the need to have in order first. To have a successful small farming business, you will need to have reliable land to grow on. Your land is a crucial component. You will need to know how much you have to work with. If you need to buy land, you will have to know where to find it and how much it will cost.

Additionally, you will want to know what crops will grow best, where, and when. You will want to consider how to create a profit from year-round crops. Then, there are rotating crops, soil, fertilizing, and so much more. Before you begin to take all of these things into consideration, you will need to know your market first. Solving all of the resource issues before you know who is going to buy from you will save you a lot of wasted effort and time.

## Setting Realistic Goals

You cannot leave things up to chance when starting your business, and what many beginners tend to do is not treat their farming endeavor as a business. If you want to generate a profit from your farm, then you will need to treat it as a business. Setting goals is a must, but simply creating a plan is still less than half of the process. Although anyone can set a goal, very few accomplish it. This is because the initial excitement they have when they start and first set their big or small goals diminishes as they start putting in the work to accomplish them. They let temptation and distraction pull them in different directions, and after a few weeks or months, their goals are long forgotten. You cannot rely on excitement alone when it comes to success. You need to have a deep internal factor that motivates you and pushes you to do the things you need to do even when you do not feel like doing them. This is what will set you apart from the hundreds of other farmers starting out.

### *Align Goals With Your Passion*

Passion is what will keep you motivated through the

ups and downs of this adventure. Without passion, you will have no purpose. Without purpose, you will let any little thing keep you from completing the priority task that will get your farm and business running. If farming is not something you are truly invested in, without profit expectation, this might not be the right course for you. You will need to be passionate about growing your own foods, taking care of the land, and seeing your efforts in a bigger scheme, such as providing food to those living in your community. You will need this passion to drive you through long, physically demanding days. This passion will get you through unexpected setbacks, like when mother nature rolls in and wipes out half your crops. Finally, you will need this passion to keep you aligned with what is most important to you instead of finding quick fixes and temporary wins.

There are many reasons why you think farming is the right path for you. However, some of the most common reasons people start their own small farming business are:

- Love for the land and farming.
- Increasing knowledge about organic foods.
- Growing your own foods for self-sufficient and sustainable living.
- Providing job opportunities or educating others.

Your reason will have a direct impact on how you set and achieve your business goals. Your "why" will be a determining factor for the processes you use on your farm and will influence daily and future operations. Before you start planning on how to layout your crops or where to sell and before you make any investment, ask yourself why it is important to have your own farm. Then ask yourself honestly if this is going to be a good enough reason to push you to put in the effort. Many people start off with the greatest intentions, but once they start putting in the work, they realize that this is not the best fit for them. Be clear about why you want to get started; think about the impact this will have on your life both now and in the future. If the desire to create change and start your own farm consistently outweighs the fears and reluctance, then this might be worth you pursuing.

If you are uncertain, then get some real-life experience working on a farm if you do not have some already. Once you know what you are getting yourself into, you will find it easier to make certain choices.

### *Set Reasonable Goals*

After you have established your "why," you need to start thinking about how you can get there. SMART goals will keep you motivated, focused, and successful. Everyone sets yearly goals and then quickly stashes them away and forgets about them. Operating a business requires you to keep your goals in focus. You should set yearly, monthly, weekly, and even daily goals. Accomplishing your daily goals will enable you to achieve your weekly goals, and conquering your weekly goals makes your monthly goals achievable. It is always important to keep your purpose in mind as you are setting your goals, both big and small. Having the end goals in mind, you will begin to create a list of goals you need to achieve to get there. For each goal you set, you will want them to meet each of the following criteria.

- Specific: Your goal must establish who is involved, what you want to accomplish, what you need to do to accomplish, and why accomplishing this is important.

- Measurable: A measurable goal gives you something to track. If you have nothing to track, you have nothing to show your progress.

- Achievable: Goals need to be realistic, within your budget, and something you are willing and able to put in the effort to achieve.

- Relevant: Goals need to relate to your purpose. There needs to be a reason for why this goal is important to achieve so that it moves you toward your desired end results. This factor is important because many people make the mistake of setting certain goals because they think they have to. Everyone else is doing it, so you must do it too. This can result in a lot of wasted time trying to achieve something that has no positive impact on what you are actually trying to gain; they just serve as a distraction.

- Timely: You will need to set a deadline to achieve your goals. Open-ended goals are often not achieved or procrastinated on. When you have a deadline, you will ensure that you are doing the things that need to be done in that timeframe.

When you have gone through all of the above, you should be left with clear and concise goals that tell you exactly what you want to achieve, how you are going to achieve them, and when it will be done. From these goals, you can create a plan that consists of small steps or milestones to accomplish daily, weekly, and monthly, so that you can make sure that all your goals will be met.

Before you start taking action on these, you will need to prioritize them. Carefully review your goals and identify the ones that have the biggest influence on your long-term goals. Also, keep in mind that you should be working on the goals that are most important to you and your well-being.

After you have prioritized your goals, you need to start taking action. This is where many begin to fail. After you have gone through the effort and daunting task of creating the goals, which may have taken more effort than you thought, you now need to put them into motion. Start with one of your top three goals. Break it down into daily manageable steps. Pick one thing you can begin doing today to help you accomplish it. Each day, choose one thing to accomplish. Once you get into the habit of making it a non-negotiable to get that one thing done, begin to choose two things, then three. As you begin to take action, remember: it is important to track your progress. Be sure to keep a record of what you are doing each day. At the end of each week, review your progress. Identify what is working for you, what you need to work on more, or what needs to be done differently. And then, with that knowledge, create a plan for the next week on how you can implement the necessary changes.

Taking this approach to your goals may seem slow. However, each task you complete will add up to your major personal or professional accomplishments. Keep in mind also that the small, consistent steps you take to start your farming business or create change will compound. Just as you cannot force a seed to grow into a fruit-bearing tree overnight, you cannot expect your goals to produce results overnight. However, if you consistently nourish that seed, provide it with water, sunlight, and the proper growing environment, eventually it will begin to grow. And from there, you will have a healthy tree-bearing fruit for weeks. Treat your goals as the seed that will flourish into the life you dream of, but they will only do so when you commit to taking care of the steps and tasks that need to be done.

# Chapter 2: Understand the Risk vs. Reward

This chapter is dedicated to helping you gain clarity over what you are getting into when you start a new business. After this chapter, we'll dive into all the ins and outs of what you need to get started, followed by the legal concerns and lending options which can be overwhelming. By first recognizing the pros and cons, you will find that all the other aspects are just part of the business. You do not want to jump into this adventure without properly assessing whether this is the best fit for you. There will be ups and downs, hard choices to make, and you may feel disappointed that your progress is not moving as quickly as you like. However, if this is something you are passionate about pursuing, these will just be hiccups in your journey.

Honestly assess what you care about getting into. You will want to ensure that a small-scale farm is something you want and will enjoy doing. You do not want to start this type of project without understanding the full commitment that needs to be made. Otherwise, you will waste time and realize too late that this is not the right adventure for you. Carefully review the information in this chapter before moving forward.

# The Pros

Farming may be in your blood, and that will make it easier to see the benefits of pursuing a farming business. If it is not, you find many aspects of owning a farm appealing. Farming is highly rewarding to those who seek a different way of living, one that allows them to set their own rules and live more independently. There are plenty of other beneficial reasons for starting your own farm as well.

## *Welcome to Entrepreneurship*

When you start and operate your own farm, you are officially a business owner. You become your own boss. As your own boss, you get to organize and establish the rules. All the control and executive decisions are made by you. Being your own boss gives you more opportunities to advance your skills, gain more experiences, and grow professionally and personally.

The work you do will be all the more satisfying despite still being hard. There is also no limitation on how much you can earn. While there is no guarantee that you will turn profits every quarter, there is also nothing standing in your way of exceeding your expected earnings. At any time, depending on the success of your farm, you can decide to give yourself a raise or a nice paid week vacation!

## *Maintain a Healthier Lifestyle*

You know that fueling your body with nourishing whole foods is beneficial to your physical and mental health.

Many people get into farming because they want to ensure that the foods they eat and feed their families are free of chemicals. Farming provides them the assurance that what they are putting into their body is of the best quality. This desire can expand to wanting to make quality fresh foods more easily available to others.

Having your own farms ensures that you always have a supply of healthy food for you and your family free of charge. Whatever you grow, you can use it for meals in your own home. There will usually never seem to be a shortage of fresh fruits or vegetables. Growing a surplus of these items lets you stay aligned with a healthy lifestyle while also making it a possibility for others too.

## *Predictable Demand*

There will always be a need for farmers and crops, and this demand is continuously growing. There are 7.5 billion people living around the world, and the global population is expected to reach 9.7 billion by 2050 (Elferink and Schierhorn, 2016). There are more people than there are farms growing food to meet the demand and need for produce. Even if you live in a small populated area, the people there are still in need of fresh produce, and you can be their supply chain. If you also take into consideration that the restaurants in your area also need fresh food supplies, rest assured that there will always be a demand for produce that your farm can definitely meet. This can take out the risk and uncertainty of whether your business will be a success. Unlike many other businesses who need to cater to a niched-down target audience and are also in competition with the next best thing, you do not have to worry about your business being taken out because of any fancy upgrades being developed. Your crops will stay as a necessity of life, and there will not be many ways you can modify or improve what you grow aside from the other items you may create with your crops like sauces or jams.

## *Easy Diversification*

When you own land, there are many options for generating an income. Growing crops and selling what you harvest is the most obvious and best-starting place. However, once you have gained the experience from a few growing seasons, you might be thinking about other ways you can expand your small farm business to create more income streams. This can be adding livestock to your farm, providing tours, allowing people to pick their own fruits and vegetables for a fee, writing cookbooks using only the crop you grow, providing an online educational resource in the form of books or a blog, selling sauces, fresh baked goods, spices, seasonings, dressing, and other homemade packaged foods. The possibilities are endless! Don't be afraid to think outside the box when looking for ways to diversify your farm, but do keep your excitement under control. You do not want to add more than you can handle or will be profitable.

## *Gratitude and Life Satisfaction*

Operating your own farm will keep you in the heart of

nature. You will witness life cycles and gain a greater appreciation for all that surrounds you. Once you have gotten through the first year and most of the fear and risk has subsided, you will reach a flow in your farming business. You'll appreciate the hard work and understand that this diligence does not just benefit you, it benefits your direct environment and community. Would you rather be sitting in morning rush hours listening to the insidious sounds of beeping horns and screeching tires, or would you rather have a fresh cup of coffee out in the field listening to the calming early sounds of nature? The work environment, co-workers, and job expectations of working on a farm are vastly different from those of a typical nine to five office job.

Every day on the job is different. While some tasks may grow mundane, you will find that you have something new to do every day. These may be new challenges to overcome or problems to solve, but no two days will be the same, and you will never get bored. Instead, you always feel like you have been productive and that what you are putting your time and energy into is serving a bigger purpose.

There is also the simple fact that most people find more satisfaction growing their own foods. You nurture your seeds from the very beginning, and in the end, you get to enjoy the product of your hard work. When you harvest your first crop and bring in a basket of fresh vegetables or fruits to create a meal, you have a greater sense of pride in your accomplishments.

### *Create Better Habits*

Those who are self-employed quickly learn that to reach their goals working for themselves, they need to have the right habits. You will quickly learn how to adopt better habits that will increase your productivity and motivation. For example, being your own boss will push you to become more disciplined and diligent because if you aren't, your business will fall. While this can be a scary thought, many farmers use this as motivation. In return, they get to enjoy a life with more flexibility and independence.

## The Cons

Though there is a lot to be gained from starting your own farm, there will be challenges. Knowing that you are going to have obstacles to overcome and being honest about your ability to stick it out and overcome them is a crucial determining factor to consider. There are many things that will be out of your control as you begin farming, and many of these things cause farmers to turn around and head back to their safer way of living. However, if you can embrace the challenges, work through them, and not let them deter you from your grand vision in life, farming may be the right business adventure to start. But, first, it is important to know what these challenges will be.

### *Mother Nature*

Mother nature is not always going to work with you, but you still need to work. Some days are going to be freezing, pouring down rain, or extremely hot. Despite what the weather is looking like that day, you will still need to get up and head to the fields. On days where the weather keeps you indoors, you will need to accept that the next day of work is going to be four times as hard and at least twice as long. You will need to be ready for disappointment when there are long days without rain or a sudden late-season frost.

You can be more adaptable to weather when you stay aware of the weather forecast. Making it a habit to check the forecast daily and prepare your farm for certain weather predictions will minimize the damage caused.

Additionally, educating yourself about the season and climate changes is essential. Having a clear understanding of when you can expect lots of rain or lack of it will allow you to begin to manage these issues well before they happen.

### *The Workday Feels Like It Never Ends*

There will be a lot of hard labour to do, especially at the beginning. Even when you are not tending to your crops, there will always be equipment needing repaired, marketing done, people to call back, and the list can feel never-ending. You might even find yourself going to bed and suddenly realizing that you've forgotten five other things. So then you'll have to get out of bed and get things done, despite being exhausted already. Starting any type of business will be demanding, but a farm is more physically and mentally draining day in and day out. Until you have established yourself and harvested your first successful crop, you will feel as if you're working 24 hours a day. However, once that crop is harvested and you see the return on your efforts, everything will be well worth it.

## *Everything Is Your Responsibility*

You are the boss. This means you will need to be aware and on top of everything before it goes wrong or gets worse. You will need to be focused and pay attention to what is going on around you. You will have to motivate yourself to work when you do not feel like it, wake up early, and work late even if you'd rather be relaxing on the couch. Farming also requires investing the time to educate yourself. Learning all the legalities and food standards is not going to be a particularly fun aspect of farming, but if you want to be successful, you will seek out opportunities to learn more about the industry. There is a lot that can go wrong, and these things can be costly. Pests can overtake your crops in a day, leaving you with nothing to harvest. Flooding can destroy your soil, so you have nothing to plant in. There are things that are going to be out of your control, but with the right planning and determination, you will remain in control of the things you can control. This will lead you to become highly successful.

## *Financial Concerns*

As you get started growing, there will be more expenses than profits. Many people who are just getting started on their farming business find themselves needing to keep their reliable day job or have to pick up a second job to pay the bills. It can be a struggle in the first one or two years to make time to complete all the farm chores. Expect a lot of late nights and early mornings. Despite the financial stress in the beginning, those who power through the first year or two agree that the struggles of the first few years were well worth it.

## Weighing Your Options

Now that you have a better idea of the pros and cons, ask yourself if this is the right fit for you. When you weigh the pros and cons against each other, the pros should significantly outweigh the cons. If you are still uncertain, you might want to try a much smaller endeavor. Having your own farm is highly rewarding and can be a profitable option to pursue, but you will need to understand that the excitement you might be feeling in the beginning will wear off once you start getting to work. Ask yourself and answer the following questions honestly before you move forward.

- Do you picture yourself maintaining your farm one year from now? Five years from now? Are you still waking up and heading to the fields every day?

- Do you have the resources to start your farm? If not, how will you find the resources? Also, be honest about how motivated you are to seek out the right resources to guarantee your farm's success.

- Are you willing to learn what is necessary for growing a successful business and farm?

- How much time are you willing to dedicate to caring for your farm?

- How long have you been waiting to start your own farming business? Is this a new interest or a passion you have been putting off for years?

- Have you ever volunteered on a farm? If not, it's a good idea to do so to get hands-on experience for what to expect.

- How much do financial gains influence your decision to start a farm? If this is the main reason, this is not going to be the right business for you.

If you still feel hesitation, it might be better to wait. Maybe you are really passionate about sustainable living and organic farming, but the amount of work it will take is not something you are willing to commit to for the long term. Maybe you have reservations about the upfront cost of starting a farm and need more time to evaluate your goals. It is understandable why you may still be uncertain about starting your own farming business, and this might come down to the fact that you do not see yourself as a business owner. Growing your own crops and making a profit does require you to shift your mindset to one that is optimistic and empowering. If you had attempted to start a crop before and did not see success, you might have adopted the mindset that you have already failed once, and you don't want to fail again. It is important that through this whole journey, you check in with yourself regularly. Be sure that your passion is still pushing you and that mistakes or unsuccessful attempts are not defining you.

Keep yourself grounded as well. Another mistake you can make when you have the idea to start your own farm is focusing too much on the big picture. It can be easy to let excitement convince you that you can take on much more than you have planned out for the beginning. You want to go big or go home right from the start. While having big goals and dreams is not discouraged, you also need to remain grounded. Wanting to jump right into having a large farm with various crops, you are going to burn out quickly and give up. Instead, start small, learn from the process, discover what works and does not work for you, and then go bigger. If you have never farmed before, there will be a lot of lessons to learn during the first few years, and you will continue learning as you continue growing. If you are willing to keep learning and growing, then a small-scale farm might be the right fit for you.

# Chapter 3:
# Gathering the Essentials

After deciding you want to move forward with your farming business, you will have to know what you need and begin to gather the tools, equipment, and other essentials necessary for operating your farm. You won't need to go out and purchase brand-new items. Starting out, you can save some of your time and money by researching on your own and buying or borrow used tools. Getting experience using certain types of equipment will help you decide what to invest in for future growth. In this chapter, there will be a wide selection of gear to acquire to get you started, but this is not an exhaustive list. You may find that as you begin, you will need other tools or equipment to make the process better suit you and your needs. The items mentioned here are suggestions, and you will have to choose whether to invest or not. But you should know what you will be investing in if you decide to do so. You need to create a budget for these items, and these items will often need some funding to help you get started.

## Land

If you do not already have much land to farm on, this is going to be the biggest part of your investment. If you are looking for land that will also serve as your residence, then it can be easier to find suitable acreage to get started, but you will have to take into account that this can result in a sizable mortgage.

If you do not have land, there are plenty of ways for you to obtain farmland. Some places to begin your search include:

- The Land Connection
- LoopNet
- Shared Earth
- Farm Lease Pro
- LandandFarm
- AgriSeek

You can also find information about land for sale or lease in your area or state by visiting the International Farm Transition Network website or FindAFarmer website. The price you pay for land will vary by location. On average, you can anticipate paying around 3,000 dollars per acre.

## Seeds

Knowing when and where to buy seeds will save you money and ensure you will have enough to get your crops started. In addition, it is important to keep in mind what season you will be growing in. Your farm will be more successful if you have a mix of cold and warm weather crops.

You need to find reputable and trustworthy seed

suppliers. You can often find a local business to purchase your seeds from, but you might find more varieties by going with an online supplier. It is important to do your research on the seller to ensure that you will get quality seeds and that they are what they are supposed to be, especially for organic seeds. Some online businesses to consider:

- American Meadows- Great selection of wildflower seeds
- Clear Creek Seed- Best for heirloom seeds, but also have vegetable, herb, and flower seeds.
- Fedco Seeds- Plenty of organic seeds options, but also has a variety of trees, vegetables, and exotic seeds.
- Pinetree Garden Seed (superseeds.com)- Offers easy-to-grow seeds, organic, heirloom, and flower seeds
- Nourse Farms- High-quality strawberry, raspberry, blackberry, and blueberry plants
- Seed Savers Exchange- Offers endangered variety seeds and rare heirloom seeds
- Seeds of Change- Nice selection of organic seeds
- High Mowing Organic Seeds- Best for certified organic seeds
- Sow True Seed- Has over 500 organic and heirloom seeds to choose from
- Renee's Garden- Best for international hybrids and exotic seeds

- Baker Creek Heirloom Seeds- Best for rare seeds
- Botanical Interests- Nice selection of all types of seeds such as heirloom, organic, and non-GMO
- Southern Exposure Seed Exchange- Best for a wide selection of tomatoes, but also has a nice selection of other vegetable seeds
- Johnny's Selected Seeds- Nice selection of high-quality vegetable and flower seeds
- Territorial Seed Company- Offers over 48 varieties of lettuce seeds and also has other vegetables, herb, and flower seeds
- Sustainable Seed Company- Great selection of vegetable, heirloom, and organic certified seeds

One important thing to keep in mind if you are buying online is to calculate the shipping fees. You will want to include these costs when you are budgeting expenses and estimating your potential profits.

Another detail to take note of is how many seeds you will be buying. You do not want to end up with an overabundance of seeds that will just go to waste and cut into your profits. On the other hand, you also do not want to short yourself and not have enough seeds to grow the right size crop to meet your expected market demand. The size of your land will help you determine how many seeds you will need to grow a profitable harvest. On average, farmers can expect to pay around 130 dollars in seeds per acre of land.

## *Seed Varieties*

If you do not have much experience growing varieties of plants, then you are going to come across some terms that will be foreign. It is important to understand your seed varieties as this will be detrimental to the production of fruits and vegetables.

Open-pollinated seeds are plants that will pollinate naturally. The wind and insects will ensure that these plants flower and are ready to harvest. These seeds are ideal because you can save seeds from your current crop to plant the next year. Another benefit of these seeds is that the plants tend to adapt better to growing conditions and climate changes each year.

Hybrid or H1 seeds are produced by professional breeders. These seeds are cultivated under controlled pollination methods, not natural pollinators. Many of these seeds are a cross of specific plant varieties that have favorable qualities like being disease-resistant or producing higher-yielding crops. While these seeds will often grow into thriving crops, if you save and reuse the seeds from one season to the next, they will not produce the same plant trait as the original. For this reason, many hybrid seed breeds are not recommended for reuse.

Heirloom seeds refer to the seeds that have been preserved from a parent plant for 40 or more years. These seeds have special genetic diversity and cultural traditions. Many heirloom varieties have distinct appearances, tastes, or characteristics that have allowed them to survive throughout the years.

Organic seeds are derived from plants that have not been exposed to pesticides, fungicides, or synthetic fertilizers. For the purpose of starting a small-scale organic garden, these are the best options. They can be more expensive than other seed varieties but will also ensure that the crops you produce are 100 percent organic.

Genetically modified organism seeds have been altered in labs. These seeds tend to be modified to incorporate specific favorable genes from various plants or to add a more desirable characteristic to an existing plant. GMO seeds are not common, and few are available for small-scale farming, but it is still wise to understand that these seeds do exist. It is more common to find non-GMO seeds.

When purchasing seeds, whether in person or online, you'll want to always check the date on the seeds. The older the date on the package, the less likely they are to germinate. It is best to purchase and use seeds meant for that year of growing.

## Tools and Gear

Having the right tools and gear from the beginning of your farming adventure will cut back on time, energy, and stress. You will need a variety of different tools, which will depend on the size and crops your farm will grow.

You will also need a few key hand tools to start your farm. Some you will use as you are working the land others will be essential for building structures, fences, and storage spaces on your land. Tools to consider include:

- Headlamp
- Basic tool kit
- Quality pocket knife
- Electric screwdriver
- Circular saw
- Jigsaw
- Reciprocating saw
- Dump cart
- Spud bar with a tamper end
- Air compressor
- Portable generator
- Ratchet straps
- Tow chain

Garden tools will be your main focus and need.

- Garden hoe
- Scythes
- Sickle
- Shovel (you will want a few different sizes for digging and planting)

- Pitchfork (this is needed for mulching)
- Garden rake
- Triller
- Weed torch (eliminate the need to spray herbicides)
- Soil blocker
- Produce scale
- Garden hose
- Weed whacker, string trimmer, or fence/hedge trimmer

You don't want to work on the farm in any old clothing. For rainy days and cold weather, you will want to have the right clothes to do your farming work in. Some items to have on hand include:

- Muck boots
- Gloves (you will need warm gloves for cold weather, durable gloves for heavy-duty work, and work gloves to keep your hands protected)
- Insulated bib overalls
- Coat
- Moisture-wicking shirts
- Hat
- Sweatband
- Dust mask

One last piece of equipment you will need to invest in for your farming business is a desktop or laptop computer. There are plenty of things you will want a dedicated business laptop for, from tracking weather when you are out in the fields to keeping accounting records and doing marketing work. It will be much easier to track progress, stay organized, and stay on track of your business goals when you have one place to keep all your business-related documents. You do not need to get the best laptop out there, but you do need to get one that will allow you to do everything you need and use it just for your farming business.

## Larger Equipment

Aside from the everyday essentials, there are a few larger pieces of equipment you should consider investing in. You will not need everything listed in this section, but you will need some. As your farm grows or you expand your crops, you may want to consider picking up a few other big pieces of machinery. These items will make your farming tasks go faster, and cutting time from these tasks can increase profits. Other items can make the process more efficient, so you can better predict and ensure a hearty harvest.

### *Tractor*

You will need a way to get around your farm, haul tools, transport crops, and move things about from one area to another. Tractors can be a huge investment but are essential for all your farming needs, so you want to choose the right one for your farming needs. When looking to purchase a tractor, keep the following in mind.

- Know how much horsepower the tractor can output. Diesel engine tractors will have more horsepower, and more horsepower means the tractor can handle more intense farming tasks.

- The type of transmission the tractor utilizes is also important. Hydrostatic transmissions are easier to operate, but it is more difficult to maintain a steady speed with them. These transmission tractors require the drive to push on the foot pedals to adjust speed. The harder you push the pedal, the faster it goes. Synchro-shift or manual gear-driven transmission requires you to use a control stick to shift gears. When shifting gears, you need to stop the tractor each time. These types of transmission allow for you to maintain a constant speed but can be more difficult to operate.

- You should know about the power take-off system (PTO). The PTO is positioned in the back of the tractor and powers the attachments used with the tractor. This system will have its own horsepower rating. The higher the horsepower, the more complex the attachments it can handle.

- To use attachments with the tracker, it needs to have a hitch. Tractors can be equipped with different types of hitches. A three-point hitch is designed with a hydraulic lift which can be used with attachments that need to be raised or lowered like a backhoe. A drawbar hitch is used for pulling different attachments. Some drawbar hitches are designed to adjust their center of gravity, even when pulling a load up or downhill. There are also specialized hitches required for front-end loader attachments and forklifts.

- Tractors can also be equipped with hydraulic power-steering systems for easier turning.

- Pay attention to the tires. Most tractor tires have exceptional traction for heavy work, but this requires the tires to be filled with a heavier fluid, not just air. Tires that can be filled with antifreeze fluid for windshield washer fluid will have more weight and better traction. Also, ensure the tractor has a four-wheel drive.

- Know the safety features of the tractor. Almost all tractors have a rollover protective structure that will keep you, or the driver, better protected in case the tractor accidentally flips or rolls.

- Not all tractors will have headlights, but these are essential for earlier farming tasks and late-day projects.

You can get a lot more use out of your tractor when you invest in the right attachment and accessories. These will speed up many farming duties and can save you from having to purchase another large piece of machinery. Some attachments to consider include:

- Cultipackers
- Harrows
- Seed Drills
- Bush hog
- Pallet forks
- Posthole digger
- Box blade
- Backhoe
- Front-end loader

Large full-sized tractors are efficient for a lot of acreages, but if you have a smaller lot of land to farm, consider a subcompact tractor. They are smaller but pack a lot of power and often have a PTO and three-point hitch, making them multi-functional. Another downsized option is a two-wheeled tractor. These tractors work with the driver walking behind the tractor. They can often be used with various attachments though the selection is limited. These units are significantly cheaper than larger, full-sized tractors. You can find a two-wheeled tractor for around 2,000 dollars.

Buying a tractor new will typically cost over 10,000 dollars. Finding a used quality tractor can cost half as much as a new one. This price is without the attachments, each of which can cost a few hundred dollars and up to a few thousand.

## *Plows*

There are many plows you can use on your farm, but not all are the same. The type of plow you need for your farm will depend on the soil and condition of the land. The crops you grow will also influence what plow you use. The most common types of plows include:

- Moldboard- These are large winged plows used to cut and turn over the soil. These should be used if the land you are farming has been untouched or out of production for a while.

- Chisel- Chisel plows will turn over soil about 12 inches deep. These plows are used to incorporate new soil that has been added to the land with older soil that has been used for crop production. This allows for the crop residue left over from the recent harvest to be shifted.

- Disk- A disk plow's purpose is to cut into the soil. This does not turn over the soil like the moldboard or chisel plows.

Most plows can be purchased for 300 dollars.

## *All-Terrain Vehicles (ATV) or Utility Vehicle (UTV)*

ATVs and UTVs are optional but can be useful to haul tools and supplies quickly. If you have a large property that your home sits on and you are using this for your small-scale farm, an ATV or UTV will get you around faster than walking. If a tractor is not within your budget, one of these vehicles can make for a great alternative. While you won't be able to use some of the more intense attachments with an ATV or UTV as you can with a tractor, they pull many of the essentials. Be sure to stick with vehicles that are designed to do more heavy work as opposed to the sporty versions meant for off-roading fun. ATVs and UTVs can be bought for as low as 1,000 dollars, but they can cost up to 10,000 dollars.

## *Pickup Truck*

You can start farming with any type of main vehicle, but a pickup truck is going to be more useful as your farm grows. Trucks will allow you to transport equipment from one location to another and haul all your tools when needed. As you begin to harvest, a pickup truck is going to be invaluable for making local deliveries. Before you trade in your compact car or SUV, you will want to know what you will need your truck for. If you only need it to haul tools from one side of your farm to another, a more sensible option would be a tractor or ATV. However, if you plan on using it for deliveries and setting up a stand at the farmers' market, it can be worth a slight investment.

Always crunch your numbers before you spend. This can be an investment you hold off on until you have a larger customer base where renting a delivery truck or van becomes a greater expense than monthly car payments. If you are mechanically efficient, you can easily find a used truck for a few thousand dollars, but they will often need a significant amount of work. If you can do the work yourself, this can be a budget-friendly option. However, a new truck will cost well over 30,000 dollars.

## *Wagon or Trailer*

A wagon can take on many shapes and sizes. This piece of equipment is attached and pulled by your tractor, ATV, UTV, or truck. Some wagons have two wheels, while others can have four or more. These are essential for hauling various items around the farm or to and from multiple locations. Thes can be purchased for around 200 dollars, but larger, more durable ones can cost over 1,000 dollars. You also have the option to build your own if you are an avid builder or if you just want to put something together for temporary use.

## *Cultivator*

Cultivators will be an essential piece of equipment on your farm. These machines cultivate the soil and prepare the land for planting. They can also be used for weed control when you adjust and properly space the times. Using a cultivator for weed control will require a steady driver as a slight shift to the right or left can take out crops you may have grown already. These machines can be hooked up to a three-point hitch on your tractor. They come in many sizes, and some are designed just for topsoil cultivation, while others are designed for deep soil tilling. If you don't mind the extra effort and do not have a lot of land to cultivate, you can find hand held cultivators that you push from behind to loosen up the soil. Heavy-duty cultivators can cost over 1,000 dollars, while handheld manual cultivators will cost a few hundred dollars.

## *Cultipacker*

These are handy pieces of equipment that will better prepare your soil for planting your seeds. This machine is pulled behind your tractor or ATV to firm the soil and allows leave grooves in the soul to prevent erosion. Once seeds are planted, you can use this to press the seeds into the soil for better contact. Cultipackers can help you maximize your crop production. Smaller ATV size cultipackers will cost around 3oo dollars. Larger cultivators can cost over 1,500 dollars.

## *Plastic Mulch Layer*

Plastic mulch layers are used in plasticulture growing methods, which lay a thin sheet of plastic mulch. An irrigation water system is set up underneath the plastic to supply efficient water to the plants. This method of growing helps with soil temperature control, moisture retention, eliminates weeds, and keeps pests from invading crops. Many farmers can take advantage of this growing method as it also allows for certain crops to be planted ahead of their typical planting seasons, such as strawberries and tomatoes. A plastic mulch layer shapes your planting beds and lays the plastic mulch along the bed.

This is a machine you want to weigh the pros and cons against. Plasticulture growing methods tend to shorten the growing allowing you to harvest much sooner. It can be the right investment, depending on the crops you plan to grow. A larger plastic mulch layer that attaches to your tractor can cost over 2,000 dollars. A smaller walk-behind or low-horsepower tractor attachment will cost a little less than 1,000 dollars. Keep in mind that you do need to have the right water irrigation system in place to work with this planting method which you will need to factor into the overall cost.

## *Irrigation System*

It will be hard to properly water your entire crop using a garden hose, so you'll need a water system in place. Your crops will need consistent water, and some crops will require more than others. Irrigation systems provide a steady and reliable stream of water to the growing field. Irrigation systems can be complex or can be simple do-it-yourself projects. Simple soaker hoses can also be used if you have the ability to connect them to an outdoor spigot. Before you install an irrigation system, you will have to know what crops you will grow and how much watering they will need daily or weekly. Some systems can be set up with multiple tiers or as an even drip system. You want to have a clear understanding of which system will work best for the crops you plan to grow. The most basic systems can be bought for a few hundred dollars. Advanced irrigation systems that also come equipped with soil moisture sensors can cost well over a thousand dollars. This seems like a pricey investment just to distribute water, but it can have a huge impact on the success of your crops.

## *Seed Drills*

Seed drills will make planting go substantially faster no matter what size farm you start. These machines plant seeds into the ground with little soil disturbances. Crop farms that require rows of seeds to be planted will benefit from these machines. Seed drills can be found as attachments for your tractor and can either be no-till or traditional. No-till drills are designed with blades that cut into the soil and break up leftover crop residue. This will create a clear line for seeds to be planted in. Traditional seed drills do not have blades that cut through the soil, so tilling and plant bed preparation needs to be done separately before planting the seeds. The sole purpose of these types of seed drills is to lay the seeds. Most seed drills will cost at least 1,000 dollars.

If you are in need of a machine that will spread the seeds out over a large area, you'll want to invest in a seeder, also known as a broadcast seeder or rotary spreader. Seed spreaders will help you grow crops and grass. The machine is used to throw out seeds over a large area that does not require the specific placement of seeds. These can be found as small manual handheld spreaders which will cost around 20 dollars. There are also large spreaders that can be attached to your tractor or pulled by your AV, which can cost up to 200 dollars.

## *Transplanter*

A transplanter will make your life easier if you have crops that need to be started indoors or as seedlings before planting into the ground. Those living in colder climates will get a great deal of use out of a transplanter. These machines will dig a hole into the ground and drop the seedling plant into the hole. These machines can be manual pieces of equipment that work by either pressing a lever with your foot or hand to drop the plant. This machine also reduces how much you have to bend over and dig or plant each seedling independently. There are also transplanter attachments that can be pulled by your tractor or ATV. These machines can cost a few thousand dollars, so be sure to honestly consider how much use you will get out of it. If you are planting on a few acres, you might be able to make do with a handheld transplanter, but for farms of ten acres, a tractor-pulled transplanter is essential.

## *Backhoe*

A backhoe is designed with a shovel arm for digging and a bucket for pushing or lifting. A backhoe attachment can be used if your tractor has a hydraulic hitch. Attachment backhoes can dig about ten feet deep. Full-sized backhoe machinery can be a useful piece of equipment if you know you will be doing a lot of digging on your land. For example, if you need to move big boulders out of the way or large clear areas of your land, a backhoe can serve you well. Backhoes can also be helpful when spreading topsoil and fertilizers or when you need to replant trees to other areas of your farm. If you can get multiple uses out of the backhoe, it can be a sensible investment, but for most, renting one may be more suitable for your budget.

There are different sizes of machines you can look into. A mini backhoe can perform many of the farming tasks you need to complete. A standard backhoe is better suited if you need to dig deeper holes greater than ten feet or have more intensive jobs you want to complete with the backhoe. Whether purchasing an attachment for your tractor or buying a mini or standard-sized machine, expect to spend 5,000 dollars for the bucket and shovel attachments and between 10,000 to 30,000 dollars for a mini or standard backhoe.

### *Front-End Loader*

A front-end loader can be a valuable asset for your farm. This machine is equipped with a bucket shovel that you will find many uses for on a daily basis. Like the backhoe, a front-end loader can be found as an attachment for your tractor, or you can find a different size loader. These will allow you to loosen up soil to prepare your land, spread soil, and fertilizer, and can be used to lift and haul heavy equipment.

An attachment piece will cost 2,500 dollars, where a mini or standard front-end loader can cost over 15,000 dollars. So if you are looking for a tractor, find a package deal that includes this equipment, and you can save yourself some money.

### *Harvester*

A harvester is not an essential piece of equipment unless you are planning on harvesting grain. Even if you are only dedicated to a small section of your land for grain, you will need a harvester. A small harvester that you walk behind can cost at least 1,000 dollars. Harvesters that need to be powered by your tractor will cost a few thousand dollars.

### *Hay Balers and Rakes*

Hay balers and rakes are also essential for specific types of farming. For example, those who are planning to produce hay will need a rake to cut the hay and a baler to roll or pack it. There are various types of each to consider, and each can be a heft investment. Combined, you can expect to pay over 10,000 dollars for this equipment. Additionally, hay balers are complex machines with various moving papers that need constant maintenance, which can add up to more than you account for in your budget.

## Outsourcing

While it is commendable to take on all the daily tasks required to get your farm up and running, this can cost you in the short and long run. You will want to maintain your excitement for starting your own business, and this will often require delegating tasks to others. Hiring farm workers is not as simple as putting anyone who is looking for a job to work or asking friends or family members to help you out. Some of the duties you might be hiring for are labor-intensive, and the person or people you will hire have to be well aware of their responsibilities. Working the land is not the only place to consider hiring for some extra help. The finances, record keeping, invoicing, marketing, and other aspects that will keep your business operating smoothly are also areas to consider letting someone else take over. Before you start looking for people to work your land, you need to have a clear idea of what tasks you will need to allocate for others to do.

Once you know what positions you need to hire for, it will be good practice to make a short list of ideal qualities, skills, and characteristics of the person or people you want to hire. These might include things like having a good job, excellent communication skills, being able to operate heavy machinery, or bookkeeping. After you list what you are looking for in your hires, you will need to calculate how much you are willing and pay for them to do the desired job descriptions.

You should have a hiring process in mind to ensure that you successfully hire the right people. During your hiring process, you should be conducting interviews to find the right person to work with. Always make it clear to the person you are interviewing what your mission is and what you are trying to achieve. Properly communicating these will help you wean out the bad seeds. Also, consider how much training you can or are willing to provide to the right candidate that shows great enthusiasm but may lack the farming knowledge you initially expected.

Do not sugar coat expectations. You need to hire people who are going to put in full effort every day. People will not give their full effort if they are led to believe that the tasks they would be doing are easy when really, they might even go without sleep, be sore from manual labor, and have to be adaptable. Set clear expectations from the very beginning, and those not fully committed will take themselves out of the pool of prospects. It is easy to weed out the people who will not be a good fit on the farm, but it can take a little creative thinking.

Those who really want the job and are excited about getting their hands dirty to accomplish the business goals you have already stated will go the extra mile to stand out.

Consider hiring on a trial period. It is not uncommon to hire someone who says all the right things during an interview and looks good on paper only to have them come to work and be completely disappointed. There are many reasons why someone may not be a good fit for your business, and it is better to let them go sooner rather than later. Let those applying for the position know that they will be hired for a trial period, for about one month, three months, six months, and at which point you will evaluate the work they have done and sit down with them to review their position.

Avoid hiring a jack of all trades. While you want to minimize your cost when hiring, you do not want to cut corners. Each person you hire should have specific duties; one person minds the water system, the other operates the planter, and everyone should know what they need to be doing. If there is any confusion, they can contact you to resolve issues.

Although farming is taxing work, you need to keep the environment upbeat and enjoyable. Otherwise, you won't have people enthusiastic about coming in for the day. Find ways to show the people you hire that you appreciate their hard work. These people can be a great asset in helping you make changes to get your business operation running more smoothly. They are the ones that can come to you with suggestions for how to streamline production, cut costs, or spot issues that hinder the growth of your crops. If they feel like they are only going to be belittled or yelled at, they are not going to come to you with solutions. Your employees will be more productive and satisfied with the work they do on your farm if you encourage them to take ownership of what they do and listen to their ideas.

What happens when you hire the wrong person? The wrong help can cost you money, time, and even your reputation. You need to address the issues as quickly as possible and either let them go or reiterate the expectation established during the interview and then let them go.

## Crafting the Right Business Plan

Though not something you need to purchase, a business plan is essential for getting started. Many people neglect to take the time to create a proper business plan, and this is why many small businesses fail to succeed or grow to their fullest potential. A business plan should be a detailed document that clearly maps out the life of your farming business. It will serve as a roadmap to follow for many aspects of your business. Before you go looking for funding, mapping out how to use your land, or purchasing any gear, create a business plan. You will need a plan to keep you focused and aligned with why you are starting this journey.

Business plans are essential for staying aligned and focused on your short and long-term business goals. To gain funding, most lenders will request a review of your business plan, and this will be a huge determining factor as to whether or not you get a loan, grants, or other types of funding for your small farm. Therefore, before you begin obtaining tools, equipment, or asking for money, you need to write a business plan. Your business plan will help guide you to what you want to accomplish with your farming business and gives you the appropriate time to work through your goals without wasting money or making unnecessary investments before you get started.

While these plans can vary in length, yours should include:

- Your business farm objectives
- Farming activities such as products or services your farm will provide
- Short and long term goals
- Estimated cost for doing business
- Expected risks or obstacles your business will face and how to overcome them
- An action plan to achieve goals
- An executive summary
- A marketing strategy
- Market research and analysis
- A description of your target market
- Knowledge of the biggest competition in your market

- Financial plan
- Clear monthly, quarterly, and annual budget breakdown
- Project growth or expansion goals

When writing a business plan, you will want to include as much detail as possible without the document becoming overly complex. Someone reading it should gain a clear understanding of the type of business you are starting, the products you will provide, the basic operations, project growth, and how you will accomplish the financial goals established. Expect your business plan to be between 15 to 20 pages long.

Your business plan will help get your business started and should be reviewed at least annually to ensure you are on track with your business goals. This document is not set in stone. You can and should update as your business grows or you decide to take your business in a new direction. It is advisable to review your business plan as a way to look at what you have accomplished, what hasn't been achieved, goals you may have lost focus on, and as motivation to continue with your small-farm business.

### *Drafting a Small Farm Business Plan*

This section will give you a better idea of how to organize and write a successful business plan for your small farm. Your business plan will be divided into sections that will include all the information mentioned previously. Your business plan will be unique and original to your values, goals, and codes of conduct. The front page of your business plan should clearly display your business name, logo, address, contact information, and a brief line that defines your business. After the front page, you should have a table of contents that lists page numbers for the executive summary, products and services, market analysis, marketing strategy, financial planning, budget, and other considerations. We will go into further detail about what each of these sections should include below. If you have applications for permits, these should be noted in the main body of the business plan and then included as appendices once the plan is completed.

**Executive Summary**

The executive summary is the first thing lenders will read when they review your business plan. The most important component of the executive summary is the mission statement. This statement is a short and concise paragraph that defines your business purpose. The mission statement takes into consideration the goals, values, and objectives of your business. When written correctly, the mission statement is what you will refer to when making a big decision about your farming business and will establish expectations for how the business should be run, the work culture. The big picture goals everyone involved is working towards.

Your mission statement should summarize what your business does, how it does it, and why it does what it is doing. This statement alone will tell investors if your business values and goals align with their own values and whether or not they want to invest in your business. It is also recommended that you add a vision statement after your mission statement. The vision statement takes the mission statement into consideration to establish a long-term goal you wish to accomplish through your business.

For example, Nike's mission statement is: "Create groundbreaking sports innovations, make products sustainably, build a creative and diverse global team, and make a positive impact in communities where we live and work" (Law, 2021). In addition, the company's vision statement is: "Bring inspiration and innovation to every athlete in the world. If you have a body, you are an athlete" (Law, 2021).

You can keep these two statements separate as their own section or combine them into a mission and vision statement section in your executive summary. While these statements are a crucial component, it is not something many businesses perfect on the first draft. It can take a few years to write a mission statement that clearly establishes your business goals and values. This statement is something you will often revisit and make adjustments to as you can gain more business experience and evaluate what is most important to you and your business operations.

If you are struggling to come up with a concise mission statement, move on to writing out the short and long-term goals for your business. Your goals should expand into five years or your business life. Use the SMART goal method to create goals that are specific, measurable, achievable, relevant, and time-sensitive. With this approach, you will be able to map out big and small wins for your business that will propel you towards a profitable and successful business.

The executive summary will also include main details about your farming business such as partners, owners or business leaders, employees, business operations, how many acres your farm is, and where it is located. You can include background information in this section to give readers a better idea of who you are. Tell them how long you have been farming or your history with farming. What type of farming techniques are you familiar with and plan to use for growing and harvesting? What environmental impact are you hoping to make with your small farm?

**Products and Services**

This section will do more than list the products or services your small farm will provide. The products and services section will also provide pricing, product lifespan predictions, production and manufacturing processes, and how customers benefit from the products supplied. This is also the section where patents acquired will be mentioned.

If you have any research and development information, you will outline it in this section as well. This section should give you and lenders the profit potentials of your small farm.

**Market Analysis**

The marketing sections are where you may spend more time researching and gathering more information. You can not expect your farm to do well if you do not have the cognizance of your target market and the farming industry. Market analysis will include information on competitors, their strengths and weaknesses, and details about customer demand. The best way to organize this section is with SWOT analysis; strengths, weaknesses, opportunities, and threats. With this analysis, you look at external and internal factors that can benefit or hinder your farming business. You will need to take into consideration various farming information and list the advantages and disadvantages of using one method over another. Here, you will list any struggles or risks your business will encounter as well as systems or ideas that can benefit your farm's entrance into the market.

**Marketing Strategy**

The marketing strategy will cover all the steps you plan to take to get your products in front of customers. You will need to describe what customers will learn about your business, how to establish a loyal customer base, and how to reach a larger audience. You will need to know what platform you will use for your advertising, customer attraction, and retention, such as advertisements, social media, and word of mouth. The more details and steps provided in the marketing strategy, the more success you will have with your marketing plan. In this section, you'll also want to decide how much money you will allocate for marketing and how exactly it will be used.

**Financial Planning**

The financial planning sections are what lenders will review thoroughly. This section should include all financial statements and balance sheets. As a new business, you won't have accurate accounts for most of this information. Instead, most of the documents here will be estimates or target price points for the first three years of your business. Also, be sure to mention potential investors in this section.

An important sub-section to include in the financial planning portion are the financial projections. They will be titled as pro formas and based on future financial expectations. Here, you will include the overall budget, not including one-time expenses. These documents are based on current market conditions and used to create a hypothetical outlook for revenues and money flow. These will also include expected market changes that will influence your business' potential to earn.

**Budget**

Creating a budget is one of the first things you need to do when starting a business, so this section should be fairly easy and quick to complete. The budget section of your business plan will list all the costs of running and maintaining your business which include daily expenses, wages, supplies, insurance, and marketing. You'll want to create a budget for your expected monthly expenses and include a budget for quarterly or annual expenses. Having a precise budget will help you uncover your true cost of business and may lead to having to make cuts to reduce spending until your farm is better established.

## Other Considerations

This last component of the business plan is optional but can be used to get a better, more defined picture of the potential you see for your farm. Other considerations can include additional drawbacks or concerns about running a small-scale farm. In addition, you can include modifications to systems or processes being implemented and highlight innovative techniques that are growing your business. This section is to provide you, partners, and lenders any additional and interesting facts or ideas you have about the growth of your business.

# Chapter 4:
# Organize the Legal Side

If you are still committed to moving forward with your farming goals, there are some key things you'll need to carefully consider first. The most important factor is funding your farm. You have just read about some of the things you will need just to get your farm started, and this may have gotten you thinking that there is no way you can pursue this type of business. There are many ways you can get funding for your farm to cover startup costs as well as to expand in the future. Knowing your options will help you feel more confident about starting your farm without having to go into serious debt.

Starting your own farming business also means there are certain legal steps you need to take to keep you and your farm protected. These are not things you want to delay taking care of because neglecting to obtain the right documents can result in not being able to sell your produce for a profit, and this can lead to huge losses.

## Do You Have Enough Funds?

As we covered in the first chapter, going into debt is not any part of the process. You will want to ensure that before you begin, you have enough money to begin cultivating and developing your crops. If you do not, you might want to postpone or have another option for obtaining the money to get started. Some ways you can secure funds for starting your farm are discussed below.

## *Grants*

Grans are the best option for getting money to cover the upfront cost of starting your small farm. Unlike other funding, you do not have to worry about repaying grant money.

There are a variety of grants available for small to mid-sized farmers, especially if you will also be provided an educational element such as teaching the community about growing food. The Specialty Crop Block Grant Program provides funding to farmers growing fruits, vegetables, nuts, and nursery plants that will be used by people. The crops can be used for food, medical purposes, or for aesthetics. These include a wide range of crops like grapes, olives, strawberries, and tomatoes. You can find a full list of eligible plants on the United States Department of Agriculture. This is a highly competitive grant, and not all states participate in the programs. It is advisable you review the information provided by the USDA website about the Specialty Crop Block Grant Program.

Additional grant programs to be aware of:

- Farmers Market Promotion Program
- Local Food Promotion Program
- Federal-State Marketing Improvement Program

- Acer Access and Development Program
- Specialty Crop Multi-State Program
- Regional Food System Partnerships

There are also additional grants available for those raising livestock on their farm. This is good to keep in mind if you plan on expanding or including sheep, cows, or chickens on your farms as well.

You will also find an extensive list of available grants on the USDA National Institute of Food and Agricultures Site. This will list what type of farm they are available for, how much funding is provided, and other details about eligibility. Additional resources to look into for grant and loan opportunities include:

- The National Sustainable Agriculture Coalition's Guide to USDA Funding for Local and Regional Food Systems
- Natural Resources Conservation Service
- The Conversation Stewardship Program
- The National Sustainable Agriculture Information Service (ATTRA)
- USDA National Agricultural Library General Funding Resource Page
- USDA Sustainable Agriculture Research and Education Program
- National Institute of Food and Agriculture Beginning Farmer and Rancher Development Program
- The Clif Bar Family Foundation

You can also look for additional funding opportunities available in your state on the National Council of State Agricultural Finance Program. If you notice your state is not listed for additional grants or loans, reach out to your State's Department of Agriculture office to learn what options are available for you.

Before you begin applying to grant programs, you need to have a well-written business plan. Most grant applications will require a document describing your farm. You will want to include information about your farm operations, the number of employees you plan to hire and their job descriptions, estimated salary for employees, operation cost, and expected revenue. Your business plan should also include an executive summary, goals, partners involved, a timeline for your farming operations, short and long-term costs, and an estimated budget.

If approved for a grant, it is imperative that you document how you have spent the money and keep records of how the money has helped you reach your farming goals. It is possible that additional funding opportunities will be provided to help you maintain your farm and future advance in your goals.

If writing a grant application is overwhelming or you do not feel you can do an adequate job of writing a grant proposal, you can hire a professional grant writer. A professional will know how to write a successful application. They may also be able to provide you information or find additional grants to apply to, or find a more secure fund for your agriculture business. Those living in the midwest of the United States can take advantage of free grant advising through the Michael Funds Agricultural Institute. Other useful resources to help with grant funding include:

- Center for Rural Affairs Farm Finances Page
- Government Grants for Small Businesses (a farm is considered a small business)
- National Council of State Agricultural Finance Programs Aggie Bonds for Beginning Farmers
- The Farmer's Guide to Agricultural Credit
- The Center for Farm Financial Management
- The Carrot Project (non-for-profit that provides resources to small and mid-sized farmers)

## *Loans*

Loans may be easier to obtain than grants and can often provide you with more funding. Obtaining a loan is dependent on your credit score and experience. These loans can be used for:

- Purchasing land
- Operating expenses
- Marketing
- Farm equipment
- Expanding operations

There are several places you can turn to for a variety of loan services for agriculture businesses. These include:

- Local banks
- Farm Service Agency (FSA)
- Housing and Community facility Program (for purchasing land)
- Farm Credit Services

You can search the National Council of State Agricultural Finance Programs website to find a list of loan programs available in your state.

To increase your approval chances, you'll want to ensure you are on good credit. Each loan opportunity will have a set of requirements to meet, and your credit score will be a huge determining factor. A credit score of 660 or above will typically put you in good credit standing.

You will also need to have your business plan available for review. The lender will want to know what they are investing in, so it is important to have a well-organized and compelling business plan.

Know the type of loan you will need. There are several different types of agricultural loans you can apply for, and each will have guidelines or requirements you must meet before approval. You need to know what these requirements are and ensure that your farm is eligible. There are also emergency loans for those who have a farm in a disaster counter or for farmers who have suffered from a 30 percent or more loss due to unfortunate circumstances.

## Increase Your Loan Acceptance

Despite there being plenty of loan opportunities for farmers and small business owners, it's very difficult to apply or access funds if you do not have proof to show your profits. However, if you are just getting started with small-scale farming, you should be able to answer a few key questions to get financing for your farm.

1. What size farm do you need to reach your financial goals?
2. Will you be operating in a small or large market?
3. Do you need to purchase land or facilities to start your farm?
4. Is there a demand for the crops you intend on growing?
5. Do you have a marketing plan? What does it look like?
6. Will you diversify your crops?

Aside from being able to answer these questions, it is crucial to have your own personal finances in order. When you are just getting started, you may have to rely on your own savings to acquire a few customers. Gaining these customers will give you some proof that your small farm has the potential to become profitable. Keep exceptional records of your business operations as you grow your customer list.

When you are ready to apply for a loan, have the following documents ready for the lender to review.

- Know how much you are going to be requesting and create a breakdown of how you will use the funds.

- Have balance sheets that show your assets, the money you are waiting to receive, and any outstanding debts you need to pay.

- Include an income statement that covers your profits and losses for the past year.

- Provide lenders with a state of cash flow.

- You will need to have proof of insurance.

- A marketing plan that details how you are going to gain customers and get your product to the customers.

- You will need to show your credit history.

**What If You Have Bad Credit?**

While it is not easy, it is still possible to get a loan when you do not meet the recommended credit score. If you have a low credit score, there are a few steps you can take to get funding for your business.

1. Look for low-credit lenders. These lenders will offer loan services, but there will be a much higher interest rate for the loan. It is important that if you choose a low-credit lender that you work to improve your credit score. Once you have a better score, you can always refinance your loan, so you get a lower interest rate.

2. Have proof of your faring experiences. Government lending programs tend to be more concerned about your farming history than with your credit score. You will need to have an impressive farming history to prove you are fit to start and operate a successful farm to be approved for a government loan, even if your credit score is subpar.

3. Find a co-signer. If you can find a co-signer that has better credit than you, you are more likely to get approved for an agricultural loan.

4. Apply for income-based loans. Loan providers may have income-based loans available. These will vary but will often have a minimum income requirement. Many farmers find they can get approved for these types of loans faster though they are often not as much as other funding options.

### *Seed Money and Angel Investors*

There is also the option to obtain seed money or find angel investors. Seed funding is usually a small amount of money that helps cover the most basic startup cost and gives your capital a boost. This funding can lead to larger funding opportunities if you can show a track record of profitability. Seed money can be obtained through crowdfunding, large companies or corporations, incubators, accelerators, venture capitalists, and angel investors.

Angel investors can be a single individual or small group of individuals willing to help companies or startups develop their business idea. They typically have an in-depth understanding of farm operations and the industry so they can be able to best gauge the success or failure of a particular person looking for funding. These lenders can include large companies, incubators, accelerators, and venture capitalists. They will offer small lending opportunities for startups at different cycles of its growth.

You will need to have a long-term plan for angel investors to consider. The more your farm grows and reaches the financial goals you have established, the more likely the angel investor will want to be a part of your success.

## Do You Have the Land?

Purchasing land is a huge investment and is the most important component for the success of your business. If you already have land, then you are well on your way to starting your own farm. If you do not have land, you need to look into obtaining some acreage to get you started, and this may require you to take out a loan to make the purchase. You can also find people who are willing to rent their land to you. You will be surprised by how many people have acres upon acres of land that are just sitting unused. These people may be willing to rent the land to you to start farming in exchange for a portion of the profits. This can be a great way to find land to start on without having to pay a huge upfront cost or worry about loan repayments. The downside to this is that you do not own the land. At any point, the person who does own the land can change what you initially agree upon or sell the property leaving you with nothing to work on. This can be especially devastating if you have put a year or more of hard work into the land.

Carefully weigh the pros and cons before you make this buying decision. Having your own land does mean greater independence and security, but it also means much greater debt.

### *Licenses and Permits*

When purchasing land, you will want to ensure that it is permitted and ready for farming. If it is not, you will have to obtain the right documents to begin farming for profit. This is also something you need to do if you already have land that you will be working on. There are certain restrictions imposed on farms that will not allow you to sell what you harvest unless you have the right legal documents to do so.

You will need to obtain the right licenses and permits to operate your small-scale farm. These can vary from state to state and be dependent on specific locations, and you will need to obtain these from both the state and federal levels.

The types of permits and licenses required will depend on your business activity and government rules. These will also impact the fees you need to pay to obtain these documents.

The U.S. Department of Agriculture makes it easy to

apply for agriculture permits. Two permits you need to consider to obtain are Plant Health Permits and Protected Plant Permits.

## Do You Need Insurance?

Your agriculture business, just like any business, will need to be properly insured. Farm insurance will protect you from the many legal issues that you will encounter during the development, growth, and lifespan of your farm. Aside from protection against injury, property damage, and product liability claims, having insurance can help you regain and recover losses due to extreme weather, pest problems, and other disasters that are out of your control. Getting the right coverage will take some research. This is not something you just want to rush through making a decision on. Below are some key factors to understand when insuring your farm.

- A standard homeowner's policy is not sufficient to cover your farming business. If you are just farming for yourself, this could be enough to protect your land but will often not cover farming equipment or machinery. For a farming business, you need to look at different policies.

- Hobby farm insurance can be obtained for those who plan to sell their produce at local farmers' markets. A hobby farm is not bigger than 500 acres wide and only has one location. Hobby farms cannot generate more than 10,000 dollars a year and cannot have staff or employees.

- You will want to consider a farm owner's insurance policy. These policies are for higher-profit generating farms, and there are many aspects of the policy that can be modified to suit your farm's needs. With farm owner's insurance, your farm is treated as a full-time place of employment and will include things like liability coverage and loss prevention.

- Do not go with a standard farm insurance policy. This is a big mistake many beginners make. They find a bundle policy that uses fixed coverage across all areas of their business. Your farm is unique, and you need to get a policy that is customized to your farm's risks and needs.

- Ensure that any structure or building on your farm is covered. Some policies will consider buildings used for farming operations (sheds, silos, or barns) as commercial buildings, and certain policies will not cover these structures.

- Know the details of what invalidates the policy. For example, it is a good idea to have fire protection included in your insurance policy, but many factors can contribute to you not being fully covered. You need to know how far hydrants or access to water needs to be in relation to buildings and fields. Covering your machinery and farm equipment is also highly recommended, but this has special guidelines for properly maintaining the equipment or risk loss of coverage if the machine needs to be repaired or replaced.

- Try to negotiate in getting the fencing on your farm included in the polity. Most policies do not cover fencing, and your farm is going to have various fences which will need regular maintenance and repairs. Getting the fencing cover can save you in the long term, but this comes at a higher premium.

- If you plan on raising livestock on your farm, you will need an additional insurance policy. Farm liability insurance will not cover damage or injury from livestock.

- Custom farming, where you are not actively involved in the dairy farming activities and instead pay someone else to operate the farm, requires a different insurance policy.

- Vehicle coverage like your tractor, ATV, UTV, or farm truck will not be covered under farm insurance. These will require you to obtain additional auto coverage, and some state it is mandatory to have these vehicles properly insured.

- If you are employing individuals to work on your farm, you need to have proper workers' compensation. The requirements vary by state. Some states make it mandatory that you have workers' compensation if the combined salary of your workers meet a minimum. Other states want you to have a policy that will protect workers from injuries obtained while on the job. Even if it is not mandatory for you to have a workers' compensation policy in effect, it is still a good choice to have one.

## Blanket vs. Individual Coverage

Two of the most common coverages you can choose from are blanket coverage or individual coverage. Blanket coverage, also referred to as unscheduled, covers all of your farm's property, including structures on the land, equipment, and livestock. This coverage lets you pay one lump sum depending on the sum of all your assets. When agreeing on this coverage, you need to have accurate calculations of your asset. Not having the correct value of your assets can lead to being underinsured, and you will not be able to make a claim due to loss.

Individual coverage, also referred to as scheduled coverage, lets you choose what assets you want to be covered and decide on an amount to be insured. This type of coverage can be better as it will allow you to prioritize assets that are of higher value.

## Crop Insurance

While farm insurance policy covers a majority of your farm operation liabilities, this doesn't protect your crops. Instead, you will need Multiple Peril Crop insurance or Crop-Hail Insurance. Multiple Peril Crop insurance is government-funded insurance, though you can obtain this insurance from private providers, rates and premiums are established by the Federal Crop

Insurance Corporation (FCIC). This insurance covers most natural disaster losses like those from drought or crop disease. This insurance, however, will not cover all types of crops. Crops that are covered include:

- Cotton
- Corn
- Wheat
- Soybeans

It is possible to ask for your specific crops to be covered if they are considered less common in your specific locations. It is vital that you ask if all your crops will be covered. Otherwise, you can suffer great losses.

Crop-Hail Insurance can be obtained from a private insurance provider. Coverage is obtained based on the acres you want to insure. You do not have to insure your entire farm. With this insurance, your crops will be protected against specific events such as damage from weather conditions like hail, extreme wind, and lightning. You may also be able to get fire protection with this policy. Unfortunately, you can not get protection from frost, drought, or excessive rain/moisture. Your farm's location will impact what you can get covered, so it is best to do thorough research on what is and is not included based on your location. You can obtain this insurance at any time of your growing season.

You can obtain both Multiple Peril insurance and Crop-Hail insurance to better protect your crops.

# Chapter 5:
# Know Your Seeds and What They'll Become

Now that you understand the beginning steps, it is time to start moving your dream of having a successful farm into a reality. Farms can be of many varieties. Will you be a vegetable farmer, grow only herbs, or have a botanical garden? Knowing what you want to grow is the first step to planning out a successful business. You do not want to be passive about this and think it will be nice to have a field of corn or an apple orchard. You'll want to be specific and clear about the type of farm you will have. This will have an impact on your potential profits as well as the other essentials you will need to get started growing.

## Choosing the Right Farm

A small farm is typically less than 180 acres, and to be successful, you will not need that much land. You can make even a small section of land work for you and your goals to become a successful farmer. What will get you to that success is a well thought out plan for the short-term so that you can begin making a profit that will lead you to the long term.

Before committing to the type of farm you want to begin, review your profit margins. Some plants will produce crops quickly. Others, like fruit orchards, will take a year before they produce a crop, and even then, there is no guarantee they will produce mature fruits. You can absolutely add these types of crops into your profit margin, but understand that this will be a long-term investment with no short-term gains.

## *Types of Farms*

Small farms can take on many forms. The most common types of farms include:

- Subsistence farms, which produce just enough food to provide for a single-family. These farms typically do not produce a surplus of produce, so there is nothing to sell for profits. Although there is no income, this type of farm can be ideal for those still unsure if they want to dive into a profitable farm venture.

- Commercial farms include any type of farm that raises or grows foods for profit, such as fish farms, dairy farms, or meat farms. Commercial farms can be the primary source of income for individuals.

- Crop farms can be a type of commercial farm but focus on growing fruits, vegetables, or grains. You can have a small crop farm that only grows one type of plant or that grows a selection of plants for profit. They can also grow different varieties of the same type of plant.

- Herb garden farms focus on growing herbs and spice plants. A herb garden can be a great addition to crop farms as many herbs can grow fast and plentiful.

- Bee farms are farms for those who want to sell bee products such as beeswax, pollen, and honey. These farms have a lower start-up cost, which makes them favorable for beginners.

- Microgreen farms are surprisingly a high-demand type of farm. Microgreens are baby plants, usually 14 days old, and have a maximum height of three feet. These plants are used for garnishes and salads in many restaurants.

- Hydroponics farms grow crops in nutrient water as opposed to in the group. These farms are favored by those who want to minimize water waste and pollution that other types of farms can cause. Since you do not need to plant in the ground, you do not need a lot of acres for a hydroponics farm. Most of these farms use a wall design to grow the plants on. These farms do require more management and can be most costly to start because you have to set up the right hydroponics systems.

- Tea gardens or farms specialize in growing plants to use for tea products. Those living in city space who want to give farming a try may achieve their dreams by having a rooftop tea garden. You will want to review building code regulations and restrictions before you start a rooftop garden.

- Mushroom farms grow a variety of mushrooms that can be grown outdoors or indoors in a better-controlled environment. Beginners may like this idea as mushrooms can be easy to grow and are typically ready for harvest in six weeks. Learning how to grow specialty mushrooms like oyster mushrooms can be more profitable as these tend to be in higher demand.

- Organic farms are usually crop farms but can also include livestock farms. These farms focus on natural and organic growing methods.

- Flower farms grow various flooring plants. This type of farm can lead to multiple and easy-to-implement diversifying opportunities. These farms can offer garden tours, supply products to local flower shops, and even work with large venues to create flower arrangements for special events.

- Fruit picking farms are farms that allow visitors to pick their own fruits. This type of farm has many benefits. You can create two different streams of income from one crop, you can harvest some of the crops yourself and sell them around your community, and you generate an income by allowing people to come and purchase what they pick themselves. By having people come to you, these farms also have lower transportation costs.

## *Profitable Crops to Consider*

**Herbs-** Herbs do not require a large space, so if you only have an acre or so, herbs can be a profitable choice. These plants tend to remain fairly small and are easy to manage. You can sell the herbs as a fresh bundle or dry them and sell them in small spice bottles. You can also have a nice selection of herbs sold in pots that people can buy and place on their countertops. You can even expand on this further by finding creative ways for people to purchase in-door herb walls or mini herb gardens, and this can be done without costing you more time.

**Bamboo-** Bamboo has many uses, making it a high-demand crop. An acre of bamboo can potentially earn you 25,000 dollars. What makes this a profitable crop is that bamboo does not require as much care or attention to grow in abundance. They can also be grown year-round and typically regrow annually. Those who want a crop that is beneficial for the environment should consider bamboo. While this crop is profitable once it gets growing, bamboo does tend to have higher start-up costs. A single plant can cost 35 dollars, and you will need quite a few to cover an acre to see a return on your investment.

**Lavender-** This flowering plant is a profitable choice because it can be sold in various ways. Lavender plants can be sold as-is. They can also be processed, and the oil can be sold, or they can be dried and sold as loose leaf tea. Selling lavender oil can bring in a revenue of 27,000 dollars, and this can be accomplished with just an acre of lavender plants. However, if you plan to process the plants yourself, you will need to consider how to properly extract the oil from the plant, and this can add up to more cost and time.

**Garlic-** Garlic is always in high demand, and garlic crops are fairly easy to maintain. They are also cold weather crops. You can plant them in the fall and harvest them at the beginning of summer. The upfront cost of getting a garlic crop started can be more expensive than other crops, but an acre can generate an income of 100,000 dollars. When you subtract the start-up cost, you are still left with over 80,00 dollars in profits.

**Microgreens-** Microgreens have a fast turnaround time and are easy to grow, and you do not need a lot of acres to grow a profitable crop. These plants can be grown indoors, so you can easily have a year-round source of income. The only downside is that your market is primarily restaurants, but with the right market plan, you may be able to appeal to other customers. You can expect to garnish 50 dollars per pound sold.

## *Seasonal Crops*

To get the most out of your farm, you need to take your location into careful consideration. Many crops will grow seasonally. Knowing which plants to grow for their ideal season will ensure you always have something to produce and bring in a profit year-round.

Understand how to read a planting calendar. A planting calendar will help you determine what crops to grow and when for the best harvest. Timing your planting is essential. For example, planting seeds that favor warm weather too early before the last frost will destroy your crop. On the other hand, planting seeds too late in the season can result in a loss of crops too, as they may not produce a crop before the weather changes again. Planting calendars simplify the planting process by dividing areas into zones and provide the best month to plant-based on the zone your farm falls into.

Most plants will be planted based on the first and last frost dates of your zone. However, after or before these dates, you can begin to understand how to stagger your crops, so you will have something to harvest throughout the entire season.

## Before You Start Planting

Before you start digging up your land, there are some essential things to keep in mind. To ensure you can begin planting as quickly as possible, be sure to have everything in order first.

### *Seeds vs. Starter Plants*

There are pros and cons to starting crops from seeds or starter plants. Each of these planting methods will require transplanting your crop into your fields or farming bed.

Starting with seeds will give you a much wider selection of plants to choose from. Buying seeds from an online catalogue will also allow you to try unique seeds that you won't find at your local nursery.

Seeds are also ideal when you are planting a large number of plants to harvest. You can save hundreds of dollars growing your crops from seeds as opposed to buying all these plants as starters.

Starting slow-growing plants from seeds indoors, early in the season, will ensure they are ready for transplant and should be ready to harvest not much long after planting in the ground. In addition, having seeds to start during the typical non-growing season will give you something to keep you busy. It can also be much more satisfying knowing that you have been caring for your crops from the very beginning. However, waiting to start long-season plants until the recommended seeding time can result in waiting much longer before the plants are ready to harvest, which can have a negative impact on your profits.

While seeds can be the best choice for beginners as purchasing the seeds can be the most cost-efficient, this does not always mean you are going to save money. To start crops from seeds, you will often start them indoors. This usually means you need a dedicated greenhouse or structure on your farm for seedlings. Depending on where you are located, you will need to invest in growing lights to ensure the seedlings are getting adequate light. Despite these upfront investments, there are usually just one-time expenses. Buying seeds each year can save hundreds of dollars every season.

Starter plants can also be beneficial because they are quick and easy to plant. You won't have to wait around for your seedling to reach a certain height or be disappointed if the seeds do not sprout. Starter plants are convenient for those who are juggling a busy schedule while trying to get their farm started.

You do not have to worry about finding the right space to keep your plants. You will be planting these right into your fields, so there is no need for an indoor space or worry about them getting enough light to flourish.

Starter plants have already progressed through the most fragile growing process. Seeds are susceptible to many diseases that will kill them off before it breaks through the soil. However, starter plants have already survived through the uncertainties and are ready to thrive in the ground.

Starter plants will require less care and maintenance. Seeds need to be hardened off, move outdoors, and after eight weeks are then ready to be planted in the ground. Starter plants will not require this extra time before you can anticipate them being ready for planting. In addition, once starter plants are in the ground, you typically do not have to wait as long as you would with seedlings before seeing your first flowering signs of fruit or vegetable growth.

If anything holds up your planning process, such as not getting the beds ready on time or a sudden late frost, you can easily push back your planting schedule. Using starter plants can get you back on your growing schedule. Since starter plants take less time until they are ready to harvest, you can actually end up ahead of schedule. This is not something you always want to do on purpose, though.

With some crops, you want to avoid both seedling and stater plant options. For example, root crops like carrots, beets, and radish fare much better when the seeds are sowed directly into the ground. Other plants that do better when started in the ground include:

- Leafy greens
- Beans
- Cucumbers
- Garlic
- Corn
- Peas
- Pumpkins
- Squash
- Okra
- Watermelon
- Eggplant
- Zucchini
- Brussels sprouts
- Cabbage
- Celery
- Poppies

There are also plants that are not grown from seeds but instead are started from root division or bulbs. These plants include:

- Artichoke
- Asparagus
- Onions
- Potatoes
- Sweet potatoes
- Rhubarb

While it is your choice whether you start from seeds or starter plants, this is a choice you need to make way ahead of planting season. Have a plan outlined for how you will get your crops started and a strategy ready to get them in the ground so that you get to harvesting successfully.

## *Planting Techniques*

Planting techniques vary from farmer to farmer and are often established through a lot of trial and error and experimentation. Each farm will yield different results when harvest time arrives due to a number of variables. Planting date, tilling practice, pests, and plant performance will all have an impact on crop growth and success, and all of these can be different from one farm to the next. You can come up with your own solid planting techniques by first getting advice from other farmers. Knowing what works and does not work with them will supply you with options. Remember, just because something does not work for them does not mean it can't work for you.

Suppose you do not have much experience yet in growing a larger crop. In that case, it is best to follow established recommendations for when to plant, what depth to plant, soil condition, and other factors that, on average, lead to healthy plant growth and germination. Once you have a grasp of what to do successfully, you can begin making adjustments to a few factors that can lead to a higher yield at harvest time. You may find that you can start your seeds a week or two earlier than recommended with no impact on harvest, except that you can harvest a little earlier. Some crops you will learn will do better being planted at a slightly deeper depth than recommended based on soil conditions and produce a better yield at harvesting. When making changes to how you plant, only doing this will be a small percent of your total crops. This will minimize your risk of losing your entire crop if the changes you make are unsuccessful. Keep track of these planting details and their results during your growing season so you can find the best times and techniques for planting.

## *Seed Placement*

There is a reason why you see stretches of farmland laid out in seemingly perfect precise rows. When you properly place your seeds or start plants in a uniform manner, you are more likely to see a more uniform harvestable crop. Seeds need to be planted at the same depth if you want your crop to emerge at the same time.

A planter can help you achieve uniformity and boost your productivity and efficiency.

When planting, placing the seeds at the right depth can make a huge difference in when seeds emerge and how much your crop produces. Seeds need enough moisture to begin the growth process. They also need a warm environment to grow in. If you plant your seeds too shallow, the soil can dry quickly and slow down the growing process. On the other hand, planting too deep and the soil temperature can be too cold, and you will not see a great yield when harvesting. Soil conditions will change from one growing season to the next, so it is important to know when you may need to plant a little deeper to ensure the seed receives enough moisture and when to plant a little shallow to ensure the seeds have enough warmth.

One final factor to be mindful of when placing seeds is referred to as closing the trench. Closing the trench means you properly place soil on top of the seed so that there is no air gap between the soil and seed. If not closed properly, this air gap will prevent moisture from reaching the seed. You need to ensure that you cover seeds adequately and then press the topsoil slightly to achieve seed-to-soil contact.

## Caring For Your Crops

No matter what type of crop you plant, all will require the same three key factors for proper growth. These are water, sunlight, and nutrient-rich soil. Not all plants require the same amount of these three items. For example, some plants need a lot of water, while some grow much better in the shade. As you gain more experience growing and harvesting your crops, you will begin to learn how to provide each crop the right mixture of these components. Two things that will hinder plant growth despite getting adequate water, sun, and nutrients are pests and weeds.

## *Pest Problems*

One of the biggest and most disruptive issues you will encounter as a farmer will be pests. Pest can include bugs, insects, rodents, deer, and birds who will feast on your crops. You need to take the necessary precautionary measures to keep your crops protected from the various pests that will destroy them. Fencing needs to be put up around the perimeter of the crop areas to keep bigger pests away, like deer. Using covers over the crops can help deter birds from swooping in and picking foods off the plants.

Insect and other bugs are more complex issues. You do not want to use harsh chemicals on your plants to keep these pests away. Anything you spray on your crops will get absorbed into the edible parts of the plant, which will then be consumed by you or your customer. Using various natural remedies is a great alternative, but many will not exclude insects that can be beneficial to your crops. Most pest determinants for keeping bugs away will keep all bugs away, the good and the bad.

### *Tackle Weeds Early*

Weeds are not only unsightly; they will steal away vital nutrients and water from the soil that your crops need to grow. Weeds can quickly become a problem and, if left unattended, will smooth out your crops, leaving you with a field of unproductive plants. Tilling your fields can help reduce weed growth before you begin planting and as your crops are growing.

Rotating crops and planting in different areas of your farm can help minimize pest and weed problems, and this can be beneficial to the soil as well. Knowing how to start your crops right under the best conditions and then nurturing them until harvest is vital for your farm's success. To maintain your farm for years to come, however, there are other elements you need to take care of. In the next chapter, you will learn that caring for your crops begins with caring for your land.

# Chapter 6:
# Caring For Your Land

You will need to ensure you have suitable land to plant in for years to come, and this requires a great deal of focus on ensuring the soil is well nourished. The hard work does not start with the plant but in the prepping prior to planting. You will have to create the right growing environment and implement the proper growing techniques to grow a successful and abundant harvest. This chapter will walk you through the various options for getting the soil ready to nourish the seeds or plants you place in the ground.

## Fertilizing Your Soil

A bountiful crop begins with healthy soil. Before you plant your first crop, you need to test the fertility levels. Having proper fertility levels before you plant is vital because once you plant, it is incredibly difficult to make adjustments to achieve better levels. Testing should be done in the early spring and late fall. Fertility levels can vary from one area of the field to another, so you should test a few areas to get a better understanding of what the soil needs to maintain higher levels of fertility. After the first initial testing, you will want to check fertility levels every three years.

During the colder months is when you want to apply a healthy layer of fertilizer to your soil. Fertilizer feeds the soil, and the soil will feed your plants. Well fertilized soil will ensure maximum crop production. This process will take trial and error and can change from year to year. How much fertilizer you, the type of fertilizer you use, and when you apply will have an impact on the soil fertility.

There are few things that can impact soil fertility levels. These include:

- Soil ecosystem
- Minerals- soil contains three core minerals; clay, sand, and silt
- Microbials

Fertilized soil will have the right balance of nitrogen, phosphorus, potassium, magnesium, and calcium. When choosing a fertilizer, you'll want to ensure it contains the appropriate levels of these nutrients. If soil contains too much or too little of these nutrients, it can be difficult to grow healthy crops. Compost is also a type of fertilizer that you can apply after you have planted your crops and while they are growing.

## Organizing Your Land

You don't want to just plant in an open field. Constructing the right setup for where you will grow will keep your crops organized and easy to find. Always start with a plan. For organizing your crops and tracking the success of your growing season, a diagram can be helpful. Draw out the lay of your land and map out where you will put each crop when they will be or have been planted, and how long before you can anticipate harvesting to start.

## *Tilling Practices*

A till is used to prepare the land for planting and can be used to turn the soil to mix old soil with fertilizer or mulch, which will add and distribute nutrients back into the soil. This process helps break up the soil, prevent weed growth, and keep pests away from crops. Tilling should not be done if conditions are too wet. This will only cause the soil to smear and will not create an adequate bed for laying seeds or planting starter plants. There are three popular tilling practices you should be aware of.

1. Conventional tillage

Conventional tillage involves multiple passes of a till through the crop field, before, during, and after the growing season. This approach to till regularly disturbs the soil and can allow for seedlings to emerge sooner than with other tilling methods. This can get your crops growing faster. Conventional tilling also uses a till to keep weeds out of hand away from growing plants until they reach a certain height.

1. Minimal tillage

This tilling practice can allow you to sow your crops sooner than conventional tillage, and crops also tend to have higher yields. This practice cuts back on tilling unless necessary or when preparing the land for sowing. Minimal tilling lowers the disruption to the soil, which can help it improve over time.

1. Zero or no-tillage

No-till farming does not use tillage to grow crops from year to year. While no-till crops do have a greater risk of being overrun with weeds, this can be more beneficial to the soil. Not tilling the land means you can sow your crops much sooner. No-till farming will also allow you to plant fall crops much sooner as you won't have to put off sowing seeds due to the soil being too wet and not doing what it is supposed to do. If using this method, there are additional measures you need to take to ensure the soil remains healthy each growing season, though this is not much different than what you should already be doing. The most important process to include with a no-till approach is crop rotation, which will be discussed a little later in this book.

Tilling can instantly improve the quality of the soil you plant in, but tilling should only be done when it is needed. Over time, excessive tiling will cause the quality of your soil to decline. This is because nutrients will be lost, and the structure of the soil will change, causing an increase in erosion.

When deciding which tilling approach to take, you should take into consideration the following:

- Soil composition
- Weeds
- Organic matter

- Water management
- Soil biology
- Crop rotation

To keep a farm successful, it is wise to adopt some no-till practice to maintain healthy land for years to come.

## *Proper Sun Exposure*

All crops will need sun exposure for proper growth. The plant's ability to absorb sunlight will depend on the surface area of the plant's leaves. Leaf disease, insects, and weeds can interfere with leaf surface area and reduce the amount of sun that the plant will absorb. Therefore, the more light it can obtain, the better the crops will grow.

Planting seeds at the right time can ensure crops get sufficient sunlight to produce a high yield for harvest time. Seeds planted earlier when days are getting longer and have more sun exposure will give crops an advantage over crops planted later in the season when longer daylight hours will only last for a few weeks before becoming shorter.

Sun exposure will impact plant temperatures. While most farmers are always concerned and pay close attention to low temperatures and frost, high temperatures will also negatively affect crop growth. If the temperature rises too much, photosynthesis can halt, resulting in low to no yield for harvesting. Therefore, during periods of high temperature, you will need to take extra precautionary steps to keep your plant temperatures at a lower temperature which can include setting up a temporary shade or misting water systems to fields.

## *Water Concerns*

Moisture plays a crucial role in seed germination. Most seeds will need 30 percent of their weight in water. Too much water and the seed will rot, while too little water and the seed will split and dry out. You will also need to ensure there is proper drainage on the land, so excess water flows away from the roots. If plant roots sit in flooded soil, the roots will begin to rot, and when the roots rot, the rest of the crop will rot too. Minerals found in the soil play a crucial role in proper water drainage. Soil that has an equal sand and clay ratio will make it easier for excess water to drain away from the crops. If the soil has too much clay, the water will sit. If the soil has too much sand, water will escape too quickly, and the roots won't have a chance to get enough water when it is needed.

Plants use water to help with the photosynthesis process but also rely on it to help keep leaf surfaces cool. Water is released through the stomata of the leaf, which reduces the heat stress placed on the leaf.

During the germination stage of plant life, it will require more water than it may have survived during the beginning, pre-germination stage. Each plant will require different amounts of water to thrive, and you will need to factor in other elements that can hinder water absorption by the roots. Once a plant has reached maturity, water absorption declines significantly.

Two main water concerns every farmer should be prepared to face are drought and flooding. Drought is when there is a serious lack of water available to the crops. Droughts can occur when temperatures remain above the expected average temperature for days, weeks, or months at a time. If there are lower precipitation levels, then a drought may occur. Severe and mild drought conditions can reduce your crop yield by 50 percent or more.

Flooding can take out your current and future crops if you do not address any issue prior to planting. While there is no way to avoid flooding when substantial amounts of rain begin to fall, or rain keeps falling down for days, there are a few things you can do to better prepare yourself and your farm for the hard hit.

First, review your farmers' insurance and check if flood damage or loss is covered. If not, ask to have it added. If the company is unable to add this to your policy, try to find another company that can.

Next, address your drainage systems. If you do not have a drainage system in place, it is time to consider one seriously. If a system is already in place, make routine checks of the system to ensure there is nothing obstructing water flow. It is common for debris and sediments to accumulate in channels and screens, which impair the system's effectiveness.

Finally, consider adding or improving water drainage systems on your farm with some of the suggestions below.

- Low-grade weirs or other water control structures
- In-ditch conservation systems
- Downstream systems
- Pipes that are designed with in-field slot
- Riser with boards to control water movement
- Upgrade or improve water infiltration systems
- Add year-round plants to slow water flow around crops
- Protect crops using sandbags or putting up temporary barriers when you know long periods of rain are about to occur

## Soil Health and Nutrition

Soil is more than just the dirt you will plant in. Soil contains minerals, water, organic matter, air, and live organisms, all of which can impact your corps. You will want to ensure that the soil is the pH for the plants you grow. pH levels are a measure of how alkaline or acidic the soil is, and this will influence the nutrients and microbes present in the soil. Most crops grow well in slightly alkaline soil because this type of environment preserves the nutrients available for plant absorption. There are plenty of ways you can supply the soil with nutrients and steps you can take to ensure healthy soil.

### *Making Your Own Compost*

Making your own compost is cost-efficient and often a more effective way to supply your crops with proper nutrients. For organic farmers, homemade compost lets you have complete control over what is going into the soil to feed your plants.

When making compost, use the dried leaves, grass clipping, and lawn debris gathered from your farm or lawn. The compost you make yourself will have a rougher quality to it than store-bought compost. This is a good sign that the compost contains living microbes that are essential for plant life and growth. A lot of the compost you buy from a supplier will have a decent amount of nutrients, but most will lack the vital microbial. Homemade compost also allows you to customize compost to include more of the nutrients the soil in your field needs, leading to higher-yielding crops. If you test your soil and notice the pH levels are too low, you can add in an alkaline matter to bring the levels up.

Homemade compost often does a much better job of slowing down or stopping soil erosion. It also adds waterways within the soil, and this prevents the topsoil of the ground from baking and cracking when exposed to too much sunlight.

Creating your own compost can also be better for the environment and help with climate control. Store-bought compost is made using large, heavy machines that use up a lot of fuel and release a lot of carbon into the atmosphere. When you make compost yourself, you are cutting back on how much fuel and energy waste goes into manufacturer compost.

**Homemade Compost Steps**

There are two types of compost you can make for your farm.

1. Cold compost uses various uncooked food scraps and organic material. These materials are placed into a large bin with a little bit of ground soil and then stored for a year. In the year time frame, the matter begins to decompose, and when it is done, you have rich compost to use on your farm.

2. Hot compost is similar to cold compost, but the process takes just a few months as opposed to a year. With warm composting, you need four main ingredients to create your material: carbon, air, water, and nitrogen. You can also create a vermicompost with this method by adding redworms or red wigglers to the compost.

You can choose to use one or both of these methods to have plenty of compost to use on your farm year-round. With hot composting, you will want to make two batches a year, one to use at the beginning of your growing season and one to make at the end.

Scrapes and matter you can use in your compost include:

- Uncooked food scraps such as fruit and vegetable peels
- Coffee grinds

- Eggshells (these should be dried and then crushed before adding to your compost bin as they can take much longer to break down than other matter)
- Grass clipping
- Dry leaves
- Plant clippings
- Finely chopped wood and bark chips
- Straw
- Untreated wood sawdust

Things to avoid using in your compost bins:

- Cooked foods
- Raw meats or poultry
- Citrus fruit peels or scraps (this can repel earthworms)
- Onion or garlic scraps (can repel earthworms)
- Foods scraps that have oil or grease on them
- Plant clippings from diseases plants
- Pressure-treated wood sawdust or chips
- Weeds that will produce seeds after they have died
- Dairy products
- Domestic animal feces (dog or cat feces)

Now that you know what you should and should not include in your composting, follow the steps below to make your own homemade compost.

For hot compost:

1. Have a large enough bin or bins to properly keep your compost. Compost bins can be essay constructed out of pallets, or you can buy large containers and bins for composting.

2. You will start with gathering enough brown material first. For hot compost that will be ready in three to six months, have at least a three-foot pile of brown material. This material will be dried grass and leaves, tree branches, bark, and other dried natural materials. This is the carbon component of your hot compost.

3. Lay green materials on top of the brown. Green materials refer to your kitchen scraps, fresh cut grass clippings, and plant trimmings. The green materials add nitrogen to your compost. When combining the brown and green material, keep it at a three to one ratio, three parts brown, one part green. You are just layering the materials at this point. You can do a few layers of each just to be sure to maintain the proper ratio of brown to green matter.

4. If the compost looks as though it contains too much moisture or is wet, add in more brown materials. If the mixture is too brown or very dry, add more green materials.

5. Water your compost regularly. Your composition should feel damp and warm but not wet. Adding too much water to your compost will cause it to rot and not decay properly.

6. You should keep track of the temperature of your compost to ensure it is not becoming too warm or wet and cold using a simple garden thermometer. Your compost should remain close to 130 degrees and not go above 150 degrees Fahrenheit.

7. When your compost does reach a temperature between 130 and 150 degrees Fahrenheit, you will need to stir it. Stirring helps minimize the odor that can occur when composting, but it also speeds up the composting process. You will continue to stir the compost at least once a week or as needed when it reaches the right temperature.

8. Your hot compost will be ready when you have a dark brown mixture that is dry and crumbling. When compost has fully cooked, the temperature should not rise, and the mixture should not be giving off heat.

For cold compost:

1. Start by setting up your compost bins or a storage area. Try to place your compost bins in a shaded area.

2. You will add material to your bins as they become available.

3. Start with dry leaves and clippings. If you have a large pile of dried leaves, do not add them all at once. Save some to layer on top of other scraps you add through the weeks. When adding kitchen scraps later, keep them towards the center of the compost bin. You do not have to worry about maintaining a certain ratio of materials.

4. As with hot compost, keep the mixture damp by adding water or fresh grass clippings. If an odor begins to waft from the bin, use a garden fork to flip the materials and allow more oxygen in.

Outdoor temperatures will have an impact on how quickly or slowly it takes for your compost to become ready. Those farming in warmer clients where the temperature stays above freezing will find their compost is ready in a short time. Farmers in colder climates, where the temperature drops below freezing overnight or in the day, will find it can take months longer for compost to be ready. Cold composting is better for those in colder climates who do not need to have compost ready or on hand for planting since there may be months where you are unable to plant.

At the beginning of your planting season, apply about six inches of compost to your fields. You can add more throughout the growing season if your soil is lacking proper nutrients.

Any leftover compost you have can be used to make a compost tea. To do this, you will use unfinished compost. Place the compost into a cloth bag. You do not want the material to escape, but you do want water to beagle to flow through the bag and the material. Place these bags of compost into a bin and fill it with water. Leave the compost to steep in the water for three days. When steeping is finished, you can use the water as a liquid fertilizer on your plants.

## *Crop Rotations*

Crop rotation is the practice of planting different crops in the same area right after each other. This is done to allow the new crop to take advantage of the residue and nutrients left behind from the previous crop. In addition, crop rotations can restore certain elements from the soil to maintain a healthy balance. For example, if you plant a crop that absorbs a significant amount of nitrogen from the soil, you will want to plant a crop after it supplies the soil with nitrogen. Many farmers use this method to help improve soil health instead of using fertilizers. This can cut back on business expenses since you do not have to spend on fertilizers as often or as much as you typically would.

Since crops will also have different root systems, planting crops with a deep roots system followed by a crop with a shallow roots system will prevent the soil from becoming depleted. This approach also helps improve drainage and water retention of the soil.

Farmers can benefit from a crop rotation plan because it allows them to consistently have something growing and ready to harvest all year round. Diversifying crops in this manner can protect you from economic hardships and a steady stream of income. This also allows you to make money and improve the physical components of the land. You may also find that consistent crop rotation produces higher-yielding crops.

## *Cover Crops*

Cover crops are plants you grow to improve the health of the soil. These crops help fertilize the soil, add organic matter, attract beneficial insects to the field, and change the nutrient value of the land. Cover crops can be planted at any time and will protect the soil from remaining bare, which will cause nutrient loss. They also help prevent weed growth and topsoil erosion. You can use these crops for long-term benefits or short-term boosts to soil health.

Long-term cover crops like oats, barley, and legumes are some of the best plants to use. Short-term cover crops should be quick-growing crops that will overpower weed growth. Buckwheat and field peas are two of the most commonly used short-term cover crops favored by farmers. The right cover crop you use will depend on a few factors such as:

- When do you next plan to plant? If you want to plant seeds right away, short-term cover crops like buckwheat are recommended.

- What types of crops will you plant? Different cover crops will release chemicals as they decompose, and this can cause certain crops to be unsuccessful when planted after the cover crop.

- Are you planting in the summer or winter? Different cover crops will be more effective depending on the season they are planted in. Clovers and Austrian pea are better for winter. Soybeans and cowpeas are better suited for summer.

When planting cover crops, you will want the plants to become as mature as possible but not mature enough where they produce seeds. Once the plant has slightly surpassed optimal maturity, kill it by mowing it or chopping it down. The crop then becomes a mulch for the land, providing it with ample food and nutrients as it decomposes.

When you are planting seeds, the temperature of the soil will have an impact on where the seed will germinate or become dormant.

### *Buffer Zones*

Buffer zones are dedicated areas of land that have permanent vegetation or flowing water. This vegetation maintains the air, water, and soil quality of the surrounding land. Buffer zones are also essential for organic farming. They provide a protective barrier for your crops against contamination or substance from infiltrating your crops.

There are no guidelines stating how big buffer zones need to be, just that they are doing their job of keeping contamination out of organic farming zones. These areas can contain any number of vegetation and are best with a diverse combination of plant life. You can grow crops for harvesting in buffer zones, though these crops will not be eligible for organic certification. The slope of the land will have an impact on buffer zone effectiveness, and this is important to consider when choosing plants to keep here.

Even if you will not intend to farm organically grown produce, it is a good idea to have buffer zones or stripes on your land. These areas provide a natural habitat for wildlife, and this can keep them away from your growing crops. Buffers can also help you maintain healthy soil throughout your land because they help control soil erosion due to wind or water. They also improve soil quality. Consider buffer zones like the shingles on your home. They provide protection and curb appeal. Once in place, they take little maintenance unless you are harvesting in the area.

## Growing and Staying Organic

If you plan on producing crops that will be labeled as organic, there are guidelines you need to follow. These guidelines are applied to the land you intend to use for your crops, soil quality, water availability, and other processes for growing and harvesting organic crops.

## *Requirements for Organic Farms*

While this is not an exhaustive list, the following requirements will help you prepare your land now for organic growing. As you implement the following requirement, you should take this time to become further educated on organic farming and best practices.

### Land Requirements

There are two major land requirements when growing organic crops.

1. The land you plan on using must be free from prohibited substances for three years. If a substance was used on your land last year and you want to grow organic tomatoes this year, you won't be able to. You will need to wait another two years before the crop would be considered organic.

2. The land needs to have buffer zones around the perimeter of the crops to protect and prevent unintentional contamination from prohibited substances. This is especially important if you have land next to other farmers that are not organic certified.

### Soil Fertility and Nutrient Requirements

Organic farmers need to take extra care of their soil and be careful how they implement traditional farming methods. Here are some things to be aware of when it comes to soil fertility and nutrient management.

- Tilling and cultivation practice must improve or at the very least maintain soil condition.

- Practice must minimize soil erosion.

- Soil management techniques cannot use chemical methods. Crop rotations, cover crops, and organic plant or animal fertilizer should be used instead.

- Farmers must be careful that crop, soil, and water contamination does not occur when using raw manure to improve soil health.

- Sewage sludge is prohibited.

- Compost must adhere to the National Organic Program (NOP) composting process guidelines.

**Seeds and Plant Requirements**

There are various rules and guidelines that deal with seeds and the types of plants that can be grown on an organic farm. While it is recommended that you familiarize yourself with the regulations, a standard rule to follow is that seeds and plants that will produce edible crops must be organic.

**Organic Crop Rotation Requirements**

Your farm must have a crop rotation plan that includes cover crops, green manure crops, catch crops, and sod crops. Crop rotation must be performed to improve the organic matter in the soil, replenish or balance plant nutrients, reduce soil erosion, and control the pest.

**Pest and Disease Management Requirements**

Integrated pest management (IPM) systems are required on organic farms. These systems are in place for pest control, weed control, and disease prevention. Practices that adhere to IPM requirements include:

- Crop rotations.
- Incorporating plant varieties on land that have a built-in resistance to pests, weeds, and disease.
- Developing a natural habitat to introduce parasites or other predators that are enemies of the pests.
- Using non-synthetic methods such as traps or lures.
- Using biodegradable mulch.
- Livestock grazing for weed control.

## *Being Certified*

To become a certified organic farm, there are a few steps you need to take to obtain the certification.

1. You must have an organic system plan. This plan outlines how your farm will operate under certified organic systems. All practices used for soil health, preparing the land, crop selection, and growing methods are key components of your plan that need to be detailed and well-organized.

2. Cet your plan review by a certified agent and begin implementing it. These agents can be found all over the world.

3. Have your farming operation inspected by a certifying agent. This will be a thorough, in-depth inspection that will review every component of your farming business and everything located on the land. The inspection will look at the field you are growing in to ensure it meets certified organic measures. It will test soil conditions and crop health. Inspecting agents will review weed, pest, and soil health management systems as well as water systems, equipment, and storage areas. Be prepared for this to be a long process.

4. Once the inspection is complete, you will want to review it with a certifying agent. The agent who did the inspection will have created thorough reports and analyses that pertain to the risk of contamination, preventative measures, and assessment of all systems in place. Another agent will review all this data and guide you to things that need to be improved, addressed, or are not in compliance with organic requirements.

5. If your farm is found to comply with all regulations, you will be issued an organic certification. Once certified, you will need to continue to update your organic system plan as you make modifications to your farm. Every

year, you will be subject to another inspection to ensure that your farm is still adhering to organic regulations. These follow-up inspections are necessary to maintain your organic certification status.

## Time Investment

Managing a farm will take a full-time commitment. Tending and caring for your crops is a time-consuming process, but there are other things you will need to spend your time on as well. For example, obtaining an organic certification will require additional effort and attention to detail. To make a profit with your farm, you will need to understand, be prepared, and be willing to put the time into daily operations.

Patience will be your greatest skill as you continue with your farming business. Knowing how to handle problems and resolve them in a timely manner will be another core skill that can lead to the success or demise of your farm. You will need to be able to properly assess when problems need to be fixed right away so you can continue with your work or step out for a day or two while you focus on something else.

# Chapter 7: Prepping Your Crop for The Market

Now that you have a clear idea of what crops you will grow, the system you will use, and have planned out your goals, you need to take a vision to your market. As mentioned earlier, growing and harvesting are only part of the farming equation. Getting your produce from the farm to the people is the other half. This requires a clear sense of your market and marketing plan and a fail-proof system for ensuring that your customer gets what they order from you. In this final chapter, we will take a look at the other essentials for building and maintaining a successful business.

## Is The Market Ready for You?

This is a crucial component of the whole process. You ideally want to ensure key factors are already in place before you begin harvesting, but if you have neglected any of the components in this section, you need to address them now.

### *Do You Have Customers?*

We discussed understanding your market when drafting your business plan, but just because there is a market does not mean you immediately have a customer base to rely on. There can be a demand for what you grow, but if no one knows that you meet their demands, you will be left with an abundance of crops and nowhere to move them.

It's crucial to build awareness around your business to attract the right customers. When you imagine the people who will buy your produce, who are they? Men, women, younger people, retired individuals? You want to know specific details about your market that will help you craft an effective marketing plan to attract these people. If you are growing various products, you might have a different audience for each product. This is important to note as you will want to have a plan in place to reach each of these markets.

## *Build an Online Presence*

If you want your farming business to take off, then it needs to have an online presence. You will need a website first to direct people to so they can learn more about your farm. If you plan on having online ordering options, you need to ensure your website is set up for eCommerce.

You also need to embrace social media. Social media is one of the easiest and fast ways you can begin to build an online presence. The potential for you to reach thousands of people is remarkable, but you need to understand the best practices for each platform. You do not need to set up an account on every platform that is available, but it doesn't hurt to create a solid presence of two or three. If you lack social media marketing skills, you can always hire someone with more knowledge and understanding to boost your presence. If it is not in your budget to hire someone, there are three general rules to follow:

1. Be consistent. You need to post every day to get more views on your profile, and some platforms favor accounts that post multiple times a day.

2. Share before you sell. A majority of what you post on your social media accounts will be about adding value to your audience, not promoting your products. As a general rule, no more than ten percent of your post should promote your business.

3. Focus on engagement. Asked questions in your post, get people to share your post with others, and always respond to comments that are left. The more engagement your post gets, the more views your profile will get.

It is best to create a social media schedule to help you stay on track with your marketing goals. Sit down once a week to map out what you will post and then create a draft of as many of these posts, so they are ready to share when you have scheduled them. Leave room in your schedule to add some live videos or images, so your profile looks and feels more authentic.

Also, consider blogging or vlogging. These avenues can provide people with more information about what you do and why. They will allow you to connect with your market on a deeper level and not just one where you are trying to sell to them. Blogs and vlogs are a great way to share your message and educate people on sustainable living. What you post through your blog or vlog will also give you more content to share on your social media accounts.

## Proper Cleaning

You need to have the proper wash system in place when you are selling your harvest. There should be wash stations located on your land so you can quickly go from harvesting to deliveries. You will want a dunk wash for leafy vegetables, which consists of tanks of water for soaking certain vegetables and gently dunking others. A spray wash system is essential for root vegetables to remove dirt. You also need a drying table to set your vegetables after washing so you are not packing them wet, which will cause bacteria and mold growth.

Using vinegar in your produce cleaning wash will remove any residue that has found its way onto the produce, either intentionally or unintentionally. It does an excellent job of breaking up wax that can build up on the outer layers of the produce. Vinegar also prevents bacterial growth, ensuring that the produce stays fresh longer.

There are plenty of ways to set up a washing station. You just need to decide what is the most efficient and effective one for you. Many farmers set up converter belts to wash root vegetables. Others have multiple soaking tanks to clean more of their harvest all at once.

You may find that these methods do not thoroughly clean the produce as they should or combine methods to save time. It does not matter which options you choose, but you do need to clean your produce before storing them or packaging them for deliveries.

## How To Sell?

Know the options you have to sell your produce. At first, you may stick with selling your crops as whole fresh fruits and vegetables. You might set up a stand at the farmers' market because this is the only available option you have. There are several ways you can sell what you grow aside from farmers' markets. There are also additional ways you can expand on what you sell. While you will need to do additional research and educate yourself further on the legal requirements, it is wise to recognize that there are plenty of opportunities to establish a successful farm in more than one way.

### *Selling Locally*

Many beginners begin to gain a loyal customer base by selling to friends, family, neighbors, and anyone else they know in the immediate community. This is a great place to get started, but it does come with a list of drawbacks and frustration. Family and friends may be eager to support you but, as human nature often is, they may expect a substantial discount or not feel pressure to pay in full when you deliver their goods. This can cause some tension within your relationships. While it is not discouraged to start this way, make sure you make it clear that you are operating a business and that your loved ones and those closest to you should treat your transaction as they would with any other business.

## *Community-Supported Agriculture (CSA)*

CSAs are subscription services that customers sign up for either as a monthly or seasonal agreement. The customer pays upfront for a percentage of the farm's harvest for the season. These subscriptions allow you to establish a great connection with your customer. The customer already pays for the crop before you even plant for the season, and these can eliminate your need to borrow money. There are a few ways you can set up successful CSAs. First, you want to start with a small customer poll. The size of your land will depend on how big this poll is. Most startup farms will do well with about 30 customers. Each customer will pay their subscription and, for the dedicated time (typically the length of the season, six or seven months), will receive their percentage of produce delivered on a weekly basis. Deliveries on average equate to around ten pounds of produce for each person.

A slightly different approach is instead of delivering the produce, the customer will come to your farm and pick up their deliveries. You can allow for items to be swapped out or traded, so customers leave with exactly what they want.

You can ensure that you grow the produce customers want by sending out a list of crops you are considering and gain feedback from these subscribers for what they would want.

CSAs are a great way to retain customers, but the biggest drawback of these is finding customers who will pay for the subscription before receiving the product.

## *Selling Wholesale*

There are many wholesale opportunities for farmers. Grocery stores, health-food stores, and other chain stores can provide you an additional outlet to sell your produce. It is not always easy to get your product or products into the wholesale arena. It can also be more stressful to guarantee and then follow through on supplying these stores with the quantity of product they expect. If you are considering going in the wholesale direction, consider consignment sales. These will often carry a higher profit.

## *Local Restaurants*

Restaurants are always in need of produce, and they can provide a great opportunity for farmers. Your best bet for landing an agreement with a restaurant is to seek out specialty locations that have staff chefs. These types of local restaurants tend to care more about using fresh whole foods in their dishes. You might struggle to find a restaurant that does not already work with a local farmer if there are plenty of farms in your area, but there will be occasions when the other farm might not come through with a delivery, and you can be the one they call. Get your name and business out and into the mix. You will also have a better chance of establishing a relationship with restaurants if you have specialty crops which can be a great selling point.

When looking for restaurants, do not be afraid to approach those in more touristy areas. These locations will have more people dining at their establishment, and the restaurants will need to make bigger orders to serve their customers, which results in better profit for you. If you do not get an immediate yes from the restaurants, you can still gain new customers by sharing with the owners and other employees other ways they can buy from you.

If you do arrange a deal with a restaurant, also ensure the produce you supply them is clean and looks good. The most important thing to keep in mind is that you have to supply what the restaurant has ordered. If you do not follow through in being able to fulfill their request for a certain quantity, they will drop you as a supplier quickly. Not receiving the full delivery can result in dishes unable to be made or only being able to make a limited number of dishes that might be one of their best selling. This costs the restaurant money. If you can not supply what you promised to deliver, then do not make the promise to do so.

## *Trade Shows and Fairs*

Trade shows and fairs are similar to a farmers' market but are a greater opportunity to promote your farm and what you supply to a larger audience. You can set up a booth to attract people to your booth, where you will have brochures, flyers, and additional ways for people to take with them how to contact you. You might even offer more than just samples of your produce or products like a cooking lesson to showcase how to create healthy and satisfying meals with your produce and products.

Chances are there are plenty of trade shows and fairs taking place in your area, and you can find out when they are happening and how to become a part of it by contacting your local chamber of commerce. Do not limit yourself to obvious farm or craft shows. Consider festivals, food fairs, and other opportunities that can get your business more attention.

To participate in most shows and fairs, you will need to pay a booth fee. These can vary from 25 dollars to over 200 dollars, and if you have to travel far to attend the show, you will have to take into consideration money spent on gas and possibly staying at a hotel since these can run late into the day. You might not make back what you put into attending these shows, so choose them carefully. If there is a greater potential for you to bring in a small profit off of items you sell, you might want to consider setting up a booth once a month or every other month.

### *Catalog Sales*

After a few years running your farming business successfully, you may have begun to branch out and started offering additional products aside from what you grow. If you have a variety of value-added products such as sauces, jams, candies, or salsa, you can create a catalog to send out or display on your website for people to order from. This venture will require more time, investment, and patience. You will need to juggle the influx of orders from the catalog, shipping the items, and often making the items on demand, and you will still need to accomplish all your normal tasks for maintaining your farm. While this option lets you use the produce you grow in different ways, and lets you use other selling options, you need to ensure you will be ready for the commitment and additional stress that can come along with selling value-adding products in this way.

## Delivering Products

While you have been busy making connections, getting businesses and the locals interested in your farming products, have you considered how you will get the product from your farm to distributors? What types of delivery services will you offer? There are plenty of opportunities to attract more customers with delivery services your farm offers, but you need to understand the commitment and obstacles that may arise by trying to do too much. A home delivery service can provide customers an easy and more convenient way to purchase your products.

### *Establishing a Delivery Service*

For home delivery options, you need to establish criteria for order placements. Before setting up guidelines for home deliveries, get feedback from your market. Ask what kind of services they would be interested in a fresh produce delivery and what things they would absolutely not be ok with. Getting feedback from your target audience will help you cater your services to what they want, which can lead to much greater success.

To help you set up a home delivery service, consider the following suggestions:

- Your website will serve as a central hub for customers to request deliveries. You need to keep your website up to date, so it provides your customer with a list of items you have or will have available for delivery.

- Be sure your website is mobile-friendly. People spend most of their time on their phones, not in front of their computers. It is important that your website is incredibly user-friendly for mobile devices.

- Create bundle delivery options. Some people love a lot of choices, but most consumers want a few options to choose from so they can order and be done.

- Consider subscription services for your deliveries. Have offers for weekly deliveries of produce that customers use often and won't keep for longer than a few days.

- Ensure your payment method requires deliveries to be paid in full at the time the order is placed. Consider adding a delivery fee to orders as well. You'll want to charge a little extra so you can cover gas and set some of the delivery revenue into a repair savings account that can be used to take care of work you may need to get done on your delivery vehicle.

- Keep your home delivery services restricted to just a small area.

- When just starting your delivery service, have set days that deliveries will take place on, like, Monday, Wednesday, and Saturday. Try to keep delivery to a time period, 12 noon to 6 pm. Once you have a comfortable handle on local deliveries, you can begin to add on more delivery locations.

Keep in mind, if you are in the process of gaining organic certifications, how you store and transport your produce will need to meet organic guidelines.

For delivery services, you will need to consider investing in delivery vans that are climate-controlled. You can make small local deliveries with your farm truck if you have proper storage and transportation systems in place. For large deliveries or when shipping to a location that is slightly further away, you will need to have the proper van to keep the produce cool, so they arrive fresh. If buying a van upfront is not an option, look into renting a delivery van instead. Know how many are available, the cost, and when you need to put in a request to ensure you have it on hand when you need it.

## Growing Your Business

Growing your farming business can take on many

forms. You can grow by focusing on gaining more customers, you can grow by offering more services or products, or you can grow by becoming more efficient in the daily tasks to run the farm.

### *Reinvesting Your Profits*

1. Once you have a handle on cultivating an easy and standard crop, consider reinvesting some of your profits to include more specialized crops.

2. Use profits to purchase equipment or machines that can speed up some of the farming processes.

3. Consider how else your land can be used. If you have a barn on the land, turning it into a bed and breakfast location can bring you in some extra money.

4. If you have spare land, consider using it for livestock or create a luxurious space to breed dogs, goats, rabbits, or other animals.

5. If you grow grapes, consider learning how to make wine to sell. This opens up a few other ways to get more out of your farm. You can offer tasting, wine classes, and tours of the vineyard. The same is true if you grow hops which you can use to make craft beers. You will need to reinvest a bit to obtain the proper machinery. If you don't have grape crops, this might be a great place to put extra funds into.

6. Reinvest profits into starting a nursery. If you have the extra land to dedicate to growing flower varieties, a nursery offers many new streams of income.

## *Expand Your Reach*

Listen to what your customers want, and then do what you can to provide it to them. Think outside the box when you visualize your ideal customer. Your target audience does not have to be limited to just one group. Take into consideration individuals who would be investing in seeing your farm grow. For example, college athletes in your area may have a greater interest in your organic product than the rest of the student body. Individuals struggling with health problems can become loyal customers if you provide them an easy way to take control of their health by choosing better foods for them. Moms of picky eaters may love your marketing ideas that speak to their picky eating kids to encourage them to eat their veggies.

Do not be afraid to embrace technology in other areas of yore farming procedures. There are apps and gadgets that will help you find imperfections in your land, give you instant solutions for crop issues, and create a better system to maximize your harvest yield. Investing some of your profits into new technology can be a smart way to see significant returns on your investment.

## *Creating Effective Systems*

Having the right operating systems in place will make running your business much easier. These systems should allow you or anyone else to complete your dairy farming tanks and other recurring obligations without hesitation. These systems are also in place to provide a backup plan when things are not going as expected, such as when weather interrupts your workday or cuts your crop in half. Operations plans will help stop a crisis from becoming out of control.

Continually educate yourself and experiment with different growing and harvesting techniques that can help you streamline your corp availability. If something works great, find ways to make it work better. If something did not work at all, find a way to make it work better. You will not always have the luxury of trying one thing, and if it does not work, move on to something different. When you are just starting your farm, you need to work with what you have, and that means making those things work in the most efficient manner.

## *Branding Yourself*

Creating a brand is the best way to ensure a loyal and long-term customer base. If you focus on having positive interactions with customers, distributors, and other merchants, more people will want to do business with you.

You will want to set your farm apart from another located in your community. To do this, you will have to look at your operations and highlight what your farm is doing differently. Establish a unique sell proposition that you can use to showcase why customers will benefit from choosing your products over others. This can reflect your mission statement.

Building a brand is about building the right reputation. What you build that reputation around depends on you. You can establish a reputation of always being friendly yet professional. Your reputation might reflect your nature and how you are always looking for ways to give back or educate the community. Your reputation may be focused on a topic that you are passionate about.

Let your passion and why guide your brand identity and reputation. People will be naturally drawn to you and your business because of your dedication and enthusiasm. If you show up consistently with that passion and drive, the market will follow. Consistency is key. Once you have established your farming business and yourself as an expert or leader of change around one topic, you need to consistently support your message.

It is important that as you are building your brand that you remain authentic in your interactions. If educating others about sustainable living and showing them how they can become more self-sufficient in their own land is not something that lights a fire in your heart, do not try to push the cause on yourself or others. Also, remember there is more to your farm and you than your mission. Let your customer and anyone else you do business with getting to know you.

# Conclusion

Farming is hard work but fulfilling work. If you can picture your life five or ten years from now, would you rather be sitting behind a desk in some office building or sitting behind the wheel of your tractor looking over endless fields of nourishing foods? If the first is more appealing to you than enjoying your comfy office chair. If the latter is what you envision, it is time to turn it into a reality.

Owning your own small-scale farm is not a side hustle. It is a full business undertaking. You need to be confident and comfortable with the time commitments required of you if you want to make a substantial profit. Be willing to embrace your farming endeavor as a learning process and be a lifetime learner. Stay up to date about the farming technologies, methods, and advancements that will lead to more profitability and less effort. This consistent effort to learn will move you from a beginner farmer to a successful farmer.

This book has provided you with an in-depth look at what it takes to start your own farming business. You have learned the tools and equipment needed to make operating your farm more efficient. You know what documents to obtain to run your business legally. You have all the information you need to go from a blank canvas of land to a self-sustaining business. Now, it is time to put this information to use.

Create a plan. Create a vision. Get up every day with passion fueling your day, and you will find the hard work rewarding in more ways than you can imagine.

We hope this book has provided you with clarity and excitement around the possibilities that can arise from starting your own small farm. We hope that you share what you have learned with others and put to use the information on these pages. If you have found value in what you learn here, we encourage you to leave a review and let others know how you have learned and grown as a farmer. We thank you and wish you luck and success on your new, exciting journey!

# References

*5 easy steps to make door-to-door delivery profitable for your farm.* (2020, April 4). BARN2DOOR. https://www.barn2door.com/blog/5-easy-steps-to-make-door-to-door-delivery-profitable-for-your-farm

*7 essential crop care tips for first-time farmers.* (2018, November 27). BARNDOOR. https://barndoorag.com/barn-blog/7-essential-crop-care-tips-for-firsttime-farmers/

*7 reasons why small farms fail.* (n.d.). Small Farm Nation. https://smallfarmnation.com/7-reason-why-small-farms-fail/

Agridirect.ie. (2018, January 3). W*hy being a farmer is the best occupation in the world.* Agri Direct. https://www.agridirect.ie/blog/why-being-a-farmer-is-the-best-occupation-in-the-world/

Anderson, S. (2016, August 26). *3 tips to successfully hire farm workers.* Farm Progress. https://www.farmprogress.com/blogs-3-tips-successfully-hire-farm-workers-11272

Arcuri, L. (2020, November 21). *Writing your own small farm business plan.* Treehugger. https://www.treehugger.com/write-a-small-farm-business-plan-3016944

B & G Garden Editors. (2020, September 9). *We've broken down the science of composting for you.* Better

Homes & Gardens. https://www.bhg.com/gardening/yard/compost/how-to-compost/

Baker, B. (2018, March 29). *How you can reduce flood risk on your farm.* Farm Progress. https://www.farmprogress.com/land-management/how-you-can-reduce-flood-risk-your-farm

*Basics of cover cropping.* (n.d.). Organic Grow School. https://organicgrowersschool.org/gardeners/library/basics-of-cover-cropping/

*Best cash crops for small farms.* (2019, September 9). Farmers Weekly. https://www.fwi.co.uk/business/business-management/best-cash-crops-for-small-farms

Bonner, M. (2019, March 28). *What types of crop insurance can you buy?* The Balance Small Business. https://www.thebalancesmb.com/what-is-crop-insurance-4178498

*Buffer strips: Common sense conservation.* (n.d.). Usda.gov. https://www.nrcs.usda.gov/wps/portal/nrcs/detail/national/home/?cid=nrcs143_023568

Campbell, L. (2021, January 17). *The modern farmer guide to buying seeds.* Modern Farmer. https://modernfarmer.com/2021/01/the-modern-farmer-guide-to-buying-seeds/

Casey. (2021, March 19). *50+ ESSENTIAL farming tools & equipment for a small farm in 2021.* Farmhacker. https://farmhacker.com/farming-tools/

Chait, J. (2019, November 20). *Organic farmland requirements.* The Balance Small Business. https://www.thebalancesmb.com/organic-farmland-requirements-2538086

*College, S. (2017, November 29).* Seed suppliers and seed catalogs for small farming. Treehugger. https://www.treehugger.com/small-farming-seed-suppliers-and-seed-catalogs-3016666

Dizon, A. (2019, August 1). *20 Most Profitable Small Farm Ideas in 2019.* Fit Small Business. https://fitsmallbusiness.com/profitable-small-farm-ideas/

*Does a farm need insurance?* (2020, July 20). Advantage Insurance Solutions. https://www.teamais.net/blog/does-a-farm-need-insurance/

Downey, L. (2020, December 13). *What is crop-hail insurance?* Investopedia. https://www.investopedia.com/terms/c/crophail-insurance.asp

Elferink, M., & Schierhorn, F. (2016, April 7). *Global demand for food is rising. Can we meet it?* Harvard Business Review. https://hbr.org/2016/04/global-demand-for-food-is-rising-can-we-meet-it

Farm and Dairy Staff. (2017, January 4). 5 tips for setting farm goals. Farm and Dairy. https://www.farmanddairy.com/top-stories/5-tips-for-setting-farm-goals/389099.html

*First time farmer loan: 3 steps to a successful loan application.* (n.d.). Upstart University. https://university.upstartfarmers.com/first-time-farmer-loan

Freedman, M. (2021, July 12). *How to qualify for an agricultural loan.* Business.com. https://www.business.com/articles/agricultural-loans/

*Funding resources for farmers (loans/grants).* (n.d.). Beginning Farmers. https://www.beginningfarmers.org/funding-resources/

Glenney, J. (2019, March 7). *Seed placement is key to ensure highest yield potential.* Farmtario. https://farmtario.com/crops/seed-placement-is-key-to-ensure-highest-yield-potential/

*Grants & Opportunities.* (n.d.). Agricultural Marketing Service U.S. Department of Agriculture. https://www.ams.usda.gov/services/grants

Gullickson, G. (2018, August 28). *11 tips for growing your farm.* Successful Farming. https://www.agriculture.com/farm-management/11-tips-for-growing-your-farm

Hayes, A. (2021, March 21). *Business plans: The ins and outs.* Investopedia.

https://www.investopedia.com/terms/b/business-plan.asp

Iannotti, M. (2021, June 12). *Should you start your vegetable garden from seeds or seedlings?* The Spruce. https://www.thespruce.com/vegetable-garden-seeds-or-seedlings-1403412

Johnson, J. K. (2017, April 19). *8 things to consider when buying a tractor.* Hobby Farms. https://www.hobbyfarms.com/8-things-consider-buying-tractor/

Kunz, L. (2016, February). *You need to be passionate about farming.* Grain SA. https://www.grainsa.co.za/you-need-to-be-passionate-about-farming

Law, T. J. (2021, June 10). *17 seriously inspiring mission and vision statement examples.* Oberlo. https://www.oberlo.com/blog/inspiring-mission-vision-statement-examples#:~:text=%20For%20quick%20reference%2C%20here%20are%2017%20examples,at%20a...%207%20TED%3A%20Spread%20ideas.%20More%20

Macher, R. (2014a, December). All about crop rotation. Grit. https://www.grit.com/farm-and-garden/crops/crop-rotation-ze0z1412zcalt

Macher, R. (2014b, December 18). *Twelve ways to sell your products.* Grit.com/. https://www.grit.com/farm-and-garden/sell-your-products-ze0z1412zcalt

McEvoy, M. (2020, December 14). *Organic 101: Five steps to organic certification.* U.S. Department of Agriculture. https://www.usda.gov/media/blog/2012/10/10/organic-101-five-steps-organic-certification

McKenzie, R. H. (2017, November 22). *Understanding the effects of sunlight, temperature and precipitation.* Top Crop Manager. https://www.topcropmanager.com/back-to-basics-20879/

Munniksma, L. (2019, October 21). *Learn the names of farm equipment & what you need.* Hobby Farms. https://www.hobbyfarms.com/names-of-farm-equipment-4/

O'Neil, T. (2021, February 5). *9 reasons you should make compost at home.* Simplify Gardening. https://www.youtube.com/watch?v=A_OATaBRUaI

Pendleton, E. (2019, April 9). *How to obtain grant money to start a farm.* Chron. https://smallbusiness.chron.com/obtain-grant-money-start-farm-17862.html

Queck-Matzie, T. (2019, December 16). *Tillage options for farmers.* Successful Farming. https://www.agriculture.com/machinery/tillage/tillage-tips

Starre, V. (2021, July 16). *Cold composting: Step-by-Step guide.* Treehugger. https://www.treehugger.com/cold-composting-step-by-step-guide-5186100

Storey, A. (2017, June 23). *What every new farmer should know about farm debt.* Upstart University. https://university.upstartfarmers.com/blog/new-farmer-farm-debt

*Suitable methods of tillage for the farm.* (n.d.). Www.fao.org. http://www.fao.org/3/y5146e/y5146e08.htm

*What is seed funding and its various types.* (n.d.). Tavaga. https://tavaga.com/tavagapedia/seed-funding/

Wickison, M. (2021, July 8). *27 ways to make money from your small farm.* ToughNickel. https://toughnickel.com/self-employment/small-farms

www.ingramcontent.com/pod-product-compliance
Lightning Source LLC
LaVergne TN
LVHW020931090426
835512LV00020B/3310